College Deans' Praise for *Eight First Choices*

HARVARD "Mitchell offers many great insig
lege admissions process and what should b
vital issue of the match between the student
—William R. F

CONNECTICUT COLLEGE "Joyce Slayton Mitchell has won my heart with this thoughtful and practical guide to the college admissions process. Her advice is straight up and free of gimmicks—a rarity found in today's college admissions resource books."

—Martha C. Merrill, Dean of Admission and Financial Aid

NORTHWESTERN "Trust Joyce Slayton Mitchell. Her advice gives everyone—students, their parents, and their counselors—the 'can do' confidence to get through college admissions without meltdown. Read this book in sections and read some of it out loud. You'll like what you hear. Ms. Mitchell knows the hearts—and minds—of students and their parents."

—Sheppard Shanley, Senior Associate Director of Admissions

CARLETON "Mitchell provides a strong personal advocacy for student decision making in the college-search process. If you can compare the search for the right college in 21st-century America to a wild, white water rafting ride, then you want this author as your river guide. There are . . . uncertainties, unseen rocks, and too many rapids among the many options facing young people in choosing a just-right college. Ms. Mitchell places the decision-making process squarely in the hands of . . . student[s] and provides the most useful tips for guiding their choice process. It is well done and [a] must read for every college-bound student."

—Paul Thiboutot, Dean of Admissions

SMITH "*Eight First Choices* makes a scientist out of the high school senior who sets out to collect data until she finds her eight perfect matches. America's vast college resources are highlighted as this book shows students how to measure all of our different campus cultures."

—Audrey Y. Smith, Dean of Enrollment

DUKE "For many years Joyce Slayton Mitchell has given outstanding advice to families seeking guidance through the college admissions maze. And we in the admissions profession have enjoyed her valuable insights, sharp opinions, and clear writing as she has examined the college selection process. This thoughtful and well-organized book, which distills her years of experience, is no exception."

—CHRISTOPH GUTTENTAG, DEAN OF ADMISSIONS

UNIVERSITY OF PENNSYLVANIA "This is the only book that puts you, as the college applicant, at the center of the admissions process. *Eight First Choices* will encourage you to be philosophical, thoughtful, and strategic about your college choices."

—ERIC J. KAPLAN, DIRECTOR, GRADUATE EDUCATION

RICE "The most interesting and practical guide I have read in many years. A 'must read' for students and parents entering the college admission process."

—RICHARD N. STABELL, FORMER DEAN OF ADMISSION

STANFORD "Joyce Slayton Mitchell is a real teacher. She uses the college selection process as a learning experience for students. She tells her students up front that they are going to learn a great deal about themselves and what's important to them. As a result, they have a much better college selection experience. For students and parents undertaking the college application process, I can think of no better guide. This book distills [Mitchell's] wisdom into 208 pages, and provides a most valuable piece of sanity and wisdom."

—ROBIN MAMLET, FORMER DEAN OF ADMISSION

EMORY "During my twenty-one years at Emory, I have benefited greatly from Joyce Slayton Mitchell's wise, accurate, and compassionate view of college admissions. Listen to what she says; she gets it right and she knows what's most important in all of this: the students!"

—SCOTT L. ALLEN, ASSOCIATE DEAN, DIRECTOR OF INTERNATIONAL RECRUITMENT

COLGATE "There are those who have been trying to sell their publications by trying to lead college-bound applicants and their families into believing that making the best college selection is as simple as reading a list or two of ill-conceived rankings. For the applicant who is serious about doing meaningful research and reading valuable suggestions about how to identify colleges and universities that could be ideal matches, Joyce Slayton Mitchell's excellent book is exactly what they should be reading. The bottom line, though, is that *Eight First Choices* is a terrific piece of work."

—GARY L. ROSS, DEAN OF ADMISSIONS

WESLEYAN "This book brings the advice of one of the great college counselors to many who need it most—and haven't typically had the advantage. You could read the first five pages and be a leg-up in the process. But don't stop there! JSM knows what she is talking about, writes clearly in an easy-to-follow format, and shares very good, practical information that will help every student be successful in making the next step to college. I have given many copies to friends and family to help pave the way for a successful college search."
— NANCY HARGRAVE MEISLAHN, DEAN OF ADMISSION AND FINANCIAL AID

POMONA "Joyce Slayton Mitchell, one of the best known experts on college admission in the United States, does it again with her third edition of *Eight First Choices*. Offering insightful guidance to college applicants, the book imparts insider knowledge sure to prove helpful to students and their families. This is a must read book by an acclaimed author."
— CHRISTOPHER S. ALLEN, DEAN OF ADMISSION AND FINANCIAL AID

BOSTON UNIVERISTY "*Eight First Choices* is the definitive guide by a leading expert in college counseling. Joyce Slayton Mitchell has advised thousands of students about the college admissions process, and her expertise and guidance will ensure that the process is seamless for you and your family."
— KELLY A. WALTER, EXECUTIVE DIRECTOR OF ADMISSIONS

INDIANA UNIVERSITY "*Eight First Choices* will provide a roadmap to the American college application process, information on how to research individual colleges and how to make sound decisions that fit you as a person based on personal and academic interests."
— MARY ELLEN ANDERSON, DIRECTOR OF ADMISSIONS

VANDERBILT UNIVERSITY "An excellent resource for parents and students alike who are trying to navigate through the college admission maze in America! This guide, through its step-by-step instructions on each component of the application process, will prove to be one of your most valuable tools. Well done!"
— DOUGLAS L. CHRISTIANSEN, PH.D., VICE PROVOST FOR ENROLLMENT MANAGEMENT AND DEAN OF ADMISSIONS

UNIVERSITY OF SOUTHERN CALIFORNIA "A wise and practical guide to outstanding American colleges and universities written by an experienced college counselor."
— JEROME A. LUCIDO, PH.D., VICE PROVOST FOR ENROLLMENT

BOSTON UNIVERSITY *"Eight First Choices* succeeds in showing the wide diversity of U.S. colleges, and thus imparts an appreciation for differences in student spirit and educational philosophy. Selecting a college because of its fuller learning environment will yield dividends in achieving those critical thinking skills that will take students as far as they want to go in their education and in their careers."

—ROBERT S. LAY, DEAN FOR ENROLLMENT MANAGEMENT

UNIVERSITY OF MICHIGAN "This book shines important new light on the issues on how and what high school students should consider when applying to U.S. liberal arts colleges and universities. Joyce Slayton Mitchell gives many practical and easy-to-follow steps to help students understand holistic admissions."

—THEODORE L. (TED) SPENCER, VP, DIRECTOR OF ADMISSIONS

WILLIAMS COLLEGE "Ms. Mitchell draws from her extensive professional experience to provide a handy roadmap for students to navigate a complex and often confusing college admission process. Mitchell's many valuable insights include a most important point of emphasis: there are hundreds of outstanding U.S. colleges and universities across the country. To receive the best undergraduate education, it is not necessary to attend the most prestigious or most highly selective of these. Look beyond artificial rankings and perceived reputation to consider a broad range of colleges with the intent to find the best match academically, socially, and financially."

—RICHARD L. NESBITT, DIRECTOR OF ADMISSIONS

8 First Choices

An Expert's Strategies for Getting into College

FOURTH EDITION

Joyce Slayton Mitchell

Eight First Choices: An Expert's Strategies for Getting into College

By Joyce Slayton Mitchell

Published by SuperCollege
2713 Newlands Avenue
Belmont, CA 94002
www.supercollege.com

Credits: Cover: TLC Graphics, www.TLCGraphics.com. Design: Monica Thomas

Layout: The Roberts Group, www.editorialservice.com

Trademarks: All brand names, product names and services used in this book are trademarks, registered trademarks or tradenames of their respective holders. SuperCollege is not associated with any college, university, product or vendor.

Disclaimers: The author and publisher have used their best efforts in preparing this book. It is sold with the understanding that the author and publisher are not rendering legal or other professional advice. The author and publisher cannot be held responsible for any loss incurred as a result of specific decisions made by the reader. The author and publisher make no representations or warranties with respect to the accuracy or completeness of the contents of the book and specifically disclaim any implied warranties or merchantability or fitness for a particular purpose. The accuracy and completeness of the information provided herein and the opinions stated herein are not guaranteed or warranted to produce any particular results. The author and publisher specifically disclaim any responsibility for any liability, loss or risk, personal or otherwise, which is incurred as a consequence, directly or indirectly, from the use and application of any of the contents of this book.

ISBN13: 978-1-61760-163-7

Manufactured in the United States of America

10 9 8 7 6 5 4 3 2 1

Library of Congress Cataloging-in-Publication Data
Names: Mitchell, Joyce Slayton, author.
Title: 8 first choices : an expert's strategies for getting into college /
   Joyce Slayton Mitchell.
Other titles: Eight first choices
Description: Fourth edition. | Belmont, CA : SuperCollege, 2020. | Summary:
   "This handbook offers general guidance to help students do a
   self-assessment and select the top eight colleges that are the strongest
   fit for them. Establishing readers as anthropologists, students will
   learn to observe 20 campus cultures, assess each one, and research their
   options in American higher education"-- Provided by publisher.
Identifiers: LCCN 2020003461 | ISBN 9781617601637 (paperback)
Subjects: LCSH: College choice--United States. | Universities and
   colleges--United States--Admission.
Classification: LCC LB2350.5 .M54 2020 | DDC 378.1/610973--dc23
LC record available at https://lccn.loc.gov/2020003461

CONTENTS

DEDICATION

For my Macau and New Zealand grandchildren,
René Mahardika Edward Mitchell, Nikau Marama Rongo
Mitchell Tei, and Zena Marama Nqakura Mitchell Tei. You are
the first generation of truly globalized students of the world.
The world-view challenge is all yours—Run with it!

ACKNOWLEDGMENTS

The primary resources for *Eight First Choices* are the voices of my college-bound students from Greenwich High School in Connecticut, Newark Academy in New Jersey, the Nightingale-Bamford School in New York City, their parents, my college advising colleagues, and the college admissions deans and reps. I am indebted to each one of them, and I am thankful that these are the particular students, parents, and colleagues from whom I have learned and with whom I work.

I am grateful also to publisher Ross Connelly, Hardwick, Vermont for the opportunity to reach out to rural college-bound students and their parents who read the "College Corner" column in the *Hardwick Gazette* and to Li Wensha, Deputy Editor-in-Chief of the China Daily's *21ˢᵗ Century Teen*, for the opportunity to reach National school students of mainland China through my college column, "College Advice USA."

With disappointed parents often at their heels, and the level of competition and stress for college admissions on a fast rise each year, it's hard for others to realize the depth of emotion and criticism that school faculty and administrators face in the reality of today's college admissions. I can never thank enough Allan E. Strand, former Headmaster of Newark Academy, for always providing me with the support necessary to work creatively under these conditions in my first independent school experience. His support provided the resources for traveling to every selective college in the country, attending the local, state, and national conferences concerned with college admissions, and hardest of all, encouraging my innovative ways to develop the college selection program at Newark Academy.

It is a pleasure to thank Kelly Tanabe, co-president of SuperCollege, for seeing the uniqueness and excitement of this book idea.

I can't imagine a career that has more rewards than working with teenagers as they learn how to create college options for their first year away from home. For living in this career, I am eternally thankful.

INTRODUCTION

··

"I had a question, but now I've forgotten it" is what I hear most often from juniors and seniors who look in my door at the College Advising Office.

"Step right across that threshold," I reply, "and I'll bet you'll remember it!" Sometimes students stand there for a minute or two before they remember two or three questions on their minds.

The second comment I hear most often from seniors is, "Ms. Mitchell, wait until I tell you my dream about getting into college! You won't believe it—I dreamed it was raining college applications!"

How on earth do you suppose the college selection process got to be such a scary task? Was it always like this? Maybe you're like the high school students I know who ask, "Isn't there some way to make it easier?" "How do I know if I want a big college or a small one?" "Should I go to one in the North or South, East or West?" "Isn't there some way to get around all of this judging and evaluating by people who don't even know me and still have some dignity left?" No, it wasn't always like this. And no, there isn't any way around being evaluated by the dean. The good news is that *Eight First Choices* will help.

After being the college counselor at two Connecticut public high schools and two private high schools (one in New Jersey and one in New York City), writing two college newspaper columns (one for the *Hardwick Gazette* in northeastern Vermont, the other a college column for the public school students of mainland China) and spending more than thirty-five years visiting and writing about college campuses, I decided to write a book for all of you college-bound high school students who want to get a handle on the process before everyone else tells you where to go to college. This book is also for those of you who don't have a counselor, teacher, or parents who know the college process. And it's for those of you who do have a college counselor but want to get the whole picture of what's going on before you go to your own guidance office to ask your questions.

I have one goal for writing this book: To help you understand the college selection process so that you will know that you are in control. Understanding the process makes it possible for you to make good decisions about where you want to go after high school. You will learn how to evaluate yourself, how to research the colleges accurately, and how to win the heart of the admissions dean by communicating and personalizing those evaluations to the colleges. Throughout the college selection process, the emphasis will be on you, a particular student looking for a special college.

Seven Basic Assumptions

Over the many years that I have worked with high school students as they have chosen their colleges, I have developed seven basic assumptions and facts that are unique to my college selection program. *Eight First Choices* is based on these seven assumptions:

1. Choose eight first choices.

You can't choose your college until the college has chosen you. In the fall of your senior year, you are establishing options for April decision making. You must choose where you hope to attend from the list of those colleges where you got in, not from where you applied. You will prioritize your college list only *after* you know the decisions the colleges have made about your applications. That's a major difference. Your family and friends often don't take this into account when they ask, "What's your first choice?" Do not prioritize your applications— think eight first choices. When others ask, name your final eight—your "eight first choices."

2. You are in charge.

The second basic assumption is that you are in charge. And that's new. Usually your parents and teachers have been in charge. They have had the last word. They know you. They know what's best for you. For the first time, you will have the last word. You are going to depend on how well you know yourself, and it's possible that some of your values are different from those of your parents and teachers. You are going to decide what is best for you.

3. Make a friend of your advocates.

People usually don't know how they make decisions. We are going to build our program around the unconscious aspects of decision making, as well as what we do know about winning the heart. No matter how you feel about them, you are going to make a friend of your guidance counselor and of the college representatives who come to your high school. Your guidance counselor will write your school recommendation to the colleges describing you to the college dean. The college dean is not going to call your favorite teacher or coach to ask them questions about your application; the dean will call your guidance counselor. You can't afford not to know—or to be less than friendly—with that counselor. Find out the name of the college admissions dean or college representative coming to your school, the so-called "designated advocate" at the college for your application. Start by knowing that person's name and how to spell it correctly. You can't afford not to know—or to be less than friendly—with your designated advocate at the college.

4. SATs and ACTs don't get you in.

No ACT or SAT score will get you in. Harvard, Stanford, Northwestern and Duke turn away about half of their 1600 perfect scores. Half. That's a lot of denial letters going out to perfect scores—but that doesn't mean that they were perfect applicants. A verbal 680 and a math 680 on your SATs won't keep you out of any college or university. Once you are in the SAT range of the colleges on your list, don't spend another hour or another dollar to raise your SATs an insignificant 20 or 30 points. Instead, spend your resources (time and money) in the classroom, on the playing fields, in the arts rooms, reading, and winning the heart of the admissions dean.

5. The college market is not a tight market.

The fifth basic assumption that students should make is that there are hundreds of colleges and universities with different campus cultures and high academic standards all over America that you will love and that are a great match for you. Every high school student who takes the college prep curriculum will find many colleges who want him or her. Contrary to what you read in the media, there is no shortage of colleges. We have more than 2,400 four-year accredited, fascinating colleges and universities in the United States. Don't get stuck on having to go to only the few that you've heard of. What you must keep in mind is that you will like best what you know best. Therefore, your task is to know several "best." Don't keep knowing one college better and better, because that's how you fall into the trap of "I've got to go to Williams and only to Williams." Ask yourself, "What is it that I like so much about Williams? What else is out there like it, with less competition for admission?"

6. Personalize the process.

The sixth and most important basic assumption of *Eight First Choices*, and for you to repeat every morning while you are brushing your teeth, is this one: There are three major steps in the college selection process: (a) assess yourself, (b) research the colleges, and (c) personalize. But the greatest of these is personalize. Personalize. Personalize!

7. Be authentically and specifically you.

The seventh and last assumption to remember is that college admissions deans are looking for ways to choose one qualified student over another. Your job is to give it to them! They are looking for authentic applicants. Find ways to express your authenticity.

When the college selection job is well done, you will have several colleges to choose from in the spring of your senior year, several campuses where you will want to go. This book will help you develop your own list of colleges with your academic record and your interests, values, and aspirations in mind. Read *Eight First Choices* thoroughly and refer to it often. Plan early, think carefully, and use all the resources available to you.

Remember that you are not in this college selection process by yourself—you're on a team. Your high school teachers, advisors, guidance counselor, principal, and coaches join you and your parents in working things out. They are your advocates. They will send your records and letters of recommendation, and they will highlight your strengths as they talk to the college admissions deans about you. They will help you gather the necessary information to make a good college decision. Therefore, while you're gathering the data about yourself and the colleges, think of it as "teamwork." You'll need advocates to help you get where you want to go. It's exciting to choose your college. It's a great adventure. Enjoy it!

How Eight First Choices Will Help

This book will expand your view of what's out there by teaching you to research the hundreds of colleges and universities in America that provide you with more options than students anywhere else in the world. It will show you the specifics that the college admissions deans are looking for, so that you will learn how to best communicate who you are and why you want to go to their colleges. *Eight First Choices* was written to give you ideas and examples you can use to describe who you are and what you want.

When I meet high school students who want to get started in the college selection process, I always begin the conversation in the same way. It doesn't matter whether they are from New York City, or northern Vermont, or Auckland, New Zealand, or Beijing, China. I start by having students tell me what kind of students they are. I want to know what they like to study, what they are looking for in a college, how independent they are, how much structure they like, how social they are, how interested they are in the performing arts, in sports, in reading. My purpose in all of these questions isn't to find "right" answers but to get them thinking in very specific terms. If a senior tells me that she swims, I ask her which events and how fast. It's not that colleges are looking for statistics in swimming, but they are looking for the particular details of those things that make you unique. Being specific and being "authentically you" are the only ways that you can separate yourself from your classmates and the rest of the applicant pool (the group of applicants applying to the same college).

> ▶▶▶ **BEING SPECIFIC AND** *being "authentically you" are the only ways that you can separate yourself from your classmates and the rest of the applicant pool.*

You are going to learn how to assess yourself as you begin to research colleges. You will make all kinds of decisions about which aspects of you to highlight on your applications. And you are going to decide which interesting specifics about your life, interests, and studies distinguish you from other potential applicants. Get ready to collect data about the different college cultures by reading about many, many colleges and listening to others talk about even more.

In November or December of your senior year, you can plan to stop collecting data about the colleges because you will decide to which colleges you are going to apply. It's then that things get even more specific. When a senior is working on his application and the question is, "Why do you want to come to Georgetown?" the answer should be tailored to that particular campus. The college dean shouldn't be able to take Georgetown out of the essay and substitute Washington University and Haverford and have it work for all three colleges. By learning to collect data on the campus cultures (life on campus), you will learn how the colleges are different one from the other. The college dean wants to know how well you know these differences. What is there about the match of that particular campus culture that you think will enable you to take advantage of the opportunities they offer you?

Learning your options is what decision making is all about. Knowing what's out there before you decide is crucial to good decision making. When the waitress asks you what kind of salad dressing you want on your salad, you have to know your options before you can choose. When your aunt asks you where you are going to college, you have to tell her that you're still researching your options before you decide.

In other words, the college selection process is a decision-making process. But unlike many other decisions, it's a tough process because it's so visible to everyone. Everybody wants to know, to compare, to judge, to give you advice and opinions. No future decision will carry as much social visibility as the college choice. Your parents, brothers and sisters, cousins, aunts and uncles, neighbors and peers will ask, "Where are you applying? Are you applying early? Isn't that a party school? What are your SATs? Did you get in?"

You and your family will often feel as if your whole identity is wrapped up in the names of the colleges to which you apply! Even though this is not true, it's easy to get carried away with this emotionally-loaded process and to forget that your identity is based on so many more things than where you go to college. For example, your identity comes from where you live, your high school experiences, your parents' occupations and income, the level of education of family members, your ethnic and religious backgrounds, your attitudes, interests, values, and ideals. Even so, never again will your decision seem so important to so many others. You will never again be asked to make a decision that everyone else in the world will know so much about. Social visibility is an extra burden of the college selection process.

Let's focus on the educational opportunities the college selection process presents. In this situation, you must learn how to distinguish yourself from your peers and create ways in which to highlight those distinguishing characteristics. This experience builds character. It will help you discover a way to think and act that you'll use all through your life. It is an opportunity to learn about yourself and to develop skills to communicate what you learn. You will get experience assessing yourself and expressing that understanding both in writing (application and essay) and in speaking (interview). Your college application and your essay are your chance to personalize and communicate your understanding of yourself in writing.

Working out your decisions at home and school, discussing your self-assessment, and learning to highlight your strengths will build your confidence. So let's agree to turn the college selection process from an emotionally loaded, no-control, anxiety-ridden experience to a positive educational experience that will provide each of you an opportunity to learn more about yourself, to learn how to research about 10 percent of America's 2,400 accredited four-year colleges from which you have to choose, and to learn how to communicate your new self-awareness to get what you want—a college environment in which you will be most productive and happy.

The College Selection Calendar

No matter when you start thinking about college, you can jump right into the selection process by looking at the following calendar. Most of you will get into some kind of formal program at school during your junior year. Or if your high school has a different college selection program, then by all means, go by your high school plan. For those of you who are starting your senior year, or even if you are halfway through your senior year, always keep in mind that it's never too late to start the process. There are some colleges that accept students all through the senior year, and others even accept students in the summer after you graduate. So…even if you've missed some of the testing deadlines, and you find yourself short on time to assess yourself and to research colleges, know that it's never too late to get into college somewhere. For those of you who are starting early—in your freshman or sophomore high school years—your curriculum choices and grades in a rigorous curriculum will have the greatest impact on your college choices.

Freshman Year

Take the most challenging courses you can successfully handle: English, algebra or geometry, Latin, a modern foreign language, and a lab science, to include five solids if you are looking for a selective college in your future. Try several different areas of activities that interest you—sports, the arts, publications, leadership in student government and clubs, and community service—to figure out your interests and talents. Plan to take your biology SAT Subject Test, and possibly math, in June at the end of your freshman year.

Sophomore Year

Continue to take the most challenging courses that you can: English, the next level of mathematics, foreign language, and science. Again, take five solids if you are still looking for a selective college. Continue with the extracurricular activities that you found fascinating and start new ones if you have time left over from your academics. Take practice PSATs in October, and a science SAT Subject Test in June. You might also want to consider taking the one in math.

Junior Year

September–June	>> Meet with college representatives
October	>> Take PSAT (all juniors)
February–June	>> Meet with your guidance counselor to discuss college list
March–April	>> Spring break: Begin college visits >> Write to your U.S. senator or representative if you are planning to apply to a U.S. military academy or participate in a ROTC program
May	>> SATs or ACTs for all juniors, AP exams
June	>> SAT Subject Tests for all juniors (three are required by many selective colleges; three should be completed by June of junior year)

| June–August | >> Visit colleges |
| | >> Write college essay draft |

Senior Year

September–November	>> Balance college list of final eight with your guidance counselor
September–December	>> Meet with college representatives
	>>College visits and interviews
	>> Student-parent college conference with counselor
October	>> Notify guidance office and teachers of early application plans
	>> Take SATs or ACTs (another chance if necessary)
November	>> Deadlines for most early applications
	>> Have teachers ready to write recommendations
	>> Register for the CSS/Financial Aid PROFILE
	>> Take SATs, ACTs if necessary
December	>> Take SAT Subject Tests if necessary (last chance for repeats of English, math, science, foreign languages)
January 1, 15	>> Deadlines for most college applications and FAFSA form
February 1	>> Deadline for many college applications, college interviews
April	>> Common college notification date
	>> Decision-making time
May 1	>> Common reply date, deposit required
	>> AP exams
June	>> Yeaaaaa!!!!! Commencement

International Students: Welcome to College USA!
Americans Abroad: Welcome Home!

International or American students coming home—colleges and universities in the USA are where students want to be! And you are just the student that the deans of admissions are looking for. Diversity is big in America. The more diversity colleges can get from all over the world, the better they like it.

If you are an international student or an American student attending an international high school or a public or national school outside the United States, and if you are familiar with admissions to universities in countries other than America, you will find the American college application process quite different. You may be surprised to know that proving your proficiency in English is not enough. Perfect test scores will not secure you a spot in an American college. American universities are concerned with far more than test scores.

Deans consider everything about you, including your special talents and service to the community. Once you are within the curriculum, grades, and test range that the colleges are looking for, they will look at who you are—the student behind all of those numbers. What is the dean looking for? He wants to know: Who is this kid? How does she think? What interests can he bring to our college campus? In fact, the application process measures your character, your ability to write, your commitment to and passion for sports, community service, and the arts. All the parts of the application process that are described in this book are the things that you must pay close attention to. The dean of admissions will want to know how you fit into his campus community and what you can contribute to the health and growth of his particular campus culture.

> ▶▶▶ **DIVERSITY IS BIG** *in America. The more diversity colleges can get from all over the world, the better they like it.*

In the American college admissions process, the international student should consider that there are more than 2,400 four-year accredited colleges and universities. Of those, there are at least three hundred excellent academically strong colleges and universities all over the country that you may never have heard of—schools that are easier to get into than the ones you happen to know about. You can begin to learn about these exceptional colleges and universities in your research through the *Fiske*, *Insider's* and *Ultimate* guides described in Chapter 3.

The *Ultimate*, *Fiske* and *Insider's* guides that describe the American colleges deal with approximately 300 to 350 colleges, that is, about 10 percent of colleges offering a baccalaureate degree. Don't get scared away because you read in the media that it's impossible to get into American colleges. If you take away the 50 colleges most competitive for admission (not necessarily the best academically, but definitely the most popular), you will still have 250 to 300 excellent and interesting colleges by any way you want to measure. These colleges can boast highly qualified professors who love to teach, a high percentage of students going on to graduate schools and top jobs in every career in the world, state-of-the-art facilities, great sports and arts programs, help with different learning styles, fabulous libraries, and high technology—all of the things that you have probably read about. What you may not know about is the depth of excellent colleges and universities we have in America, and that there is plenty of room for many more international students. In fact, many deans of admission travel around the globe describing for you the reasons why you should consider coming to their campuses in all locations of America.

For Americans coming home from the Leysin American School in Switzerland, the International School of Beijing, the International School Singapore, the American School of Paris, the English-speaking Merchiston Castle School in Edinburgh, Abbotsleigh in Sydney, the Diocesan School in New Zealand or the Ukarumpa International School in Papua New Guinea, you should seek help from your high school guidance counselor who knows what colleges the graduates before you have attended and can make suggestions that will aid you in your research. Even though you have been abroad and don't feel up to date with the college scene, still, no matter what, you will be confident of your English-speaking competencies. Use this book to learn how to research America's great array of colleges and universities and to add the personalized application approach to better your chances for admission to your final eight choices.

Lucky for you, college admissions tests—the SATs, ACTs, and the SAT Subject Tests—are given in 180 countries all over the world. If you go to a national school in mainland China and do not have access to the SATs, many American colleges will waive the requirement for you as they know that you are not able to take them in the People's Republic of China. Other colleges accept APs in place of SATs from mainland China who do not offer SATs. Follow the guidelines in Chapter 2 for which tests to take when. If English is not your first language, you may be required to take the Test of English as a Foreign Language (TOEFL) or the International English Language Testing System (IELTS). One of these is required by almost all of the colleges and universities in the United States. Each college is different in their admissions test requirements. It will be your responsibility to check with each college to which you apply and ask for the testing requirements. The TOEFL is offered online and the IELTS is offered in 500 test centers, including mainland China, around the world on 48 different dates. One of the major differences in the two tests is that the IELTS is a paper-based test and requires a face-to-face interview for the spoken English section. Check www.toefl.org and www.ielts.org for registration and detailed information.

Many colleges have a cutoff point for the IELTS and the TOEFL. Write or email the dean of admissions to learn what the cutoff point is at the schools to which you will be applying. For example, you must have a computer-based TOEFL score of 250 or a 7 on IELTS to get into Columbia, a 213 or 6.5 to get into Colorado College, and a 173 or a 6 to get into the University of Oregon. This should give you an idea of the variation at three colleges.

As soon as the testing is out of the way, you will want to carefully read Chapter 8 on writing the very important essay, and Chapter 9, which talks about filling out the application. Recommendations may be new to you, and when you read this section in Chapter 9, notice what it is that the dean wants to learn about you from these letters. College letters of recommendation should be from people who know you well, not the big shots that know your parents well. The deans want to hear what your classroom teacher has to say about your learning style and your leadership in the classroom. Letters from coaches and the performing arts teachers should describe at what level you perform in athletics or the arts—as well as your sense of responsibility, leadership, and character. Before you give the recommendation form to your teachers, show them the teacher recommendation section in Chapter 9, so that they will see in what areas the dean of admissions wants to learn more. Remember that you have to win the heart of the admissions dean from afar—remember too, it can be done!

> ▶ ▶ ▶ **HOW YOU FINANCE** *your education is a concern you will want to raise early in the application process if you are dependent upon American money to attend a college in the United States.*

Financial aid is definitely different for international students than it is for U.S. citizens. In fact, many colleges have a cap on how much financial aid they can offer to international students. Read Chapter 6—College Economics 101. How you finance your education is a concern you will want to raise early in the application process if you are dependent upon American money to attend a college in the United States. For example, many universities give a maximum amount of money in financial aid to international students and others give no money at all to international students. On the other hand, financial aid to international students has changed drastically in the past year. For the first time, several colleges are not distinguishing between American and international students for meeting the financial need of the student. Middlebury College, Mount Holyoke, and the University of Pennsylvania, for example, are among those colleges. Yale University has a "need-blind" admissions policy to all foreign students seeking undergraduate degrees. Duke significantly increased their financial aid to international students. Globalization has hit the financing of university education in America. Keep in mind, however, that accepted students must always document their ability to pay before they are accepted, no matter whose money it is.

U.S. laws for visas vary from country to country. The student visa situation has tightened for international students. It is important to realize that a student visa will not permit you to work in the United States. You will need a green card (U.S. government document) to prove permanent residency if you intend to work, although most of you will not be residents. Again, you have to check the visa laws according to what country you are from. Once you have been accepted by the college, the college will give you good advice on how to get your student visa. Look at it this way: It would be highly unusual for an international student not to be able to get a student visa once he or she has been admitted to an American college.

Think about the information you need about the college to which you are applying in order to have a successful American experience. Find out if there are classes in English as a Second Language (ESL) offered on campus. If ESL classes are offered, ask how soon you can begin these classes. Check to see if there are special housing considerations for international students. Most of you will want to be sure that you have campus housing before you get here. The college dormitories are where you will get to know the other students on a daily, informal level. Find out if there are special programs, clubs, and counseling for international students. Ask if there is a dean of international students so that you will know where you can direct your questions.

Americans returning home: Your parents may still work and live abroad, but chances are that you've got aunts and uncles, grandparents and cousins in the United States. Write ahead to them and be sure they know you are coming. It may not sound cool now while you're still at home with your parents, but by the time you are settled in and want a plan and some place to go for Thanksgiving, your relatives may look a lot better to you.

PART I

Developing Your College List

CHAPTER 1

SELF-ASSESSMENT

You are in charge. Now what's being in charge going to mean to you? What does "knowing what's best for you" have to do with the college selection process? Between now and January 1 of your senior year, you are going to figure out who you are, what you want, what colleges are out there, and how to win the heart of the college admissions dean (after you decide to which colleges you want to apply, of course). Does that make sense? No one does a good job at anything if the task doesn't make sense to them. So, that's it. You are in charge, and every step has to make a lot of sense to you so that you always put your best foot forward. In fact, you need to jump in with *both* best feet!

In order to do your best in the college selection process, you have to know that it is a three-step procedure: self-assessment, college research, and communication. The first step is a self-assessment, or evaluation of your academic standing, your educational values, interests, and aspirations. You will use this assessment when you discuss colleges with your guidance counselor, your mom and dad, and your friends; when you write your college applications; and when you go for your college interviews. Rice University's former Dean of Admissions cautions you to "be honest with yourself in your assessment." Don't kid

3

yourself about the record you are "going" to have; look at the record that you have now as you evaluate yourself.

Goals and Values

Think about it. Go beyond what kind of student your teachers say you are and express by their grades and comments. Get past what your parents—and your big sister—think about you as a student. Which subjects do you love or hate to study? How much time do you put in when you don't like the teacher? Could you be working more? Do you want a college where you can take it easier than you have in high school? Or do you want college courses that will challenge you?

Think about the questions below and add some of your own:

➢ What kind of student am I?

➢ What kind of student would I like to become?

➢ What aspects of high school have I enjoyed the most?

➢ What parts of school do I like the least?

➢ How do I define success?

Students at my school have to work really hard. On the other hand, the work ethic is high and the majority get into it. They learn to love working hard. That means that after attending classes all day, and taking part in sports or plays or music after school, they get home around 6:30 or 7:00 and they have a minimum of three hours of focused homework. They often work their heads off and come up with Bs and Cs. No one at our school gets all As. Well, almost no one. Some years one student will end up with all As and A minuses.

When I meet them as juniors I say, "Think about the college environment you want. What kind of kids do you want to be around? Who are your kind of people?" No curious student is happy at a college that doesn't have serious students. Even C and D students in some schools are intellectually curious, and they don't want a college where parties and sports are top priority. On the other hand, I point out to students that they may not want to keep on working as hard in college as they did in high school. They might want to spend more time with their peers, in the arts or sports, or just hanging out for a change. In other words, don't assume that you want the same environment that you are used to, your older siblings want, your best friends want, or your parents want for you.

There's an important book that will be very interesting for many of you to read as you think about what kind of student you are and want to become. It's called *Colleges That Change Lives* and was written by Loren Pope. Consider what Pope says: "You're not as smart as you think you are if you believe: 1. Your college should be bigger than your high school. 2. A name-brand college will give you a better education and assure you success. 3. A university will offer you more than a good small college." His book goes on to describe forty fascinating campus cultures that accept B and C students and produce graduates who make a difference in the world. You want to find the college that is right for you, and it may not be the one that is at the top of everyone else's list.

As I first meet a new class of juniors, I talk about all of these things. I ask each of them to write a one-page introduction of themselves and give a copy to their college advisor, the person with whom they will be working until they get through the early, regular, or late-decision admissions process. (See Chapter 9.) If you want to get started on this first step in decision making, go ahead, write a one-page description of what kind of student you are. Leave out your grades and talk about what you like and don't like to study. Everything you write will be grist for the mill. Those college applications and interviews are looking for your assessment of yourself. Knowing your goals and values will go a long way toward writing your application and winning the hearts of the college deans.

Academics

It is crucial for you to understand your academic standing in the college selection process. You should have a pretty good idea of what kind of a student you are and what your "numbers" are by the time that you make your final list of potential colleges. When counselors and college reps talk "numbers," they mean the strength of your high school curriculum, grades, class rank, and your SAT or ACT and PSAT scores. If a college is on your final list, it's there because you've got the numbers—that is, you are academically qualified to go there. The best strategies in the world won't get you in if you don't have the numeric standing that a college requires. Also remember that at very selective colleges highly qualified students are denied by the hundreds. Ivy deans often frighten their audiences when they tell them that Columbia, Harvard, and Princeton turn away more than half of the valedictorians who apply. Valedictorians! Answer these questions to help you assess yourself in terms of academics:

> What are my favorite and least favorite courses?

> What do I choose to learn when I learn on my own?

> Do my grades reflect my ability and potential? Why or why not?

> How well has my high school prepared me for college?

> Are my SAT scores an accurate measure of my ability?

> What is the average number of hours I study each night?

We are talking here about winning the heart of the college deans for qualified students, where as few as 5.6 percent (Harvard and Stanford) or where 7 to 12 percent of qualified students may get in (Columbia, Princeton, Yale, Brown, California Institute of Technology, Massachusetts Institute of Technology). You will need to use all of your time, energy, and money winning the heart of the dean at a college where you <u>do</u> have the numbers, so don't even think of winning a heart where you don't qualify.

There are always a few students in every class who think that even though they don't yet have the grades and SATs that Ivy league schools demand, they are so exceptional in other ways that they will get in. And it's very easy to find people who will take your time and money to affirm your belief. After all, you must remember that getting into college is big business in America. When someone is going to help you, notice if she is from your high school, an alumna or alumnus of the college, an SAT tutor or private consultant, and if the advice comes from a profit or nonprofit source. No matter who tells you what's best for you in your college admissions process—or any other decision such as traveling abroad, choosing a movie, or buying CDs—always notice what's in it for them to give you that advice. While we are on that subject, let's address one more thing: always keep in mind that the college admissions office is the marketing arm of the college. They are after as many applications as they can get. Like coaches, they throw a wide net, but their interest is their institution. Your high school teachers' and your parents' interest is you. Of course the college representatives, professors, and deans are friendly and helpful and want you to apply—that's their job!

Now, where were we? Oh yes . . . applying to college without the numbers. Let me tell you a story: No matter what I said, Jamie was sure that Amherst would take him because he was so crazy about the school. No one could possibly want to go to school there more than Jamie! As his college advisor, I could see that he was so far off base that he and his parents received one of the very few letters I send home to say that he was using poor judgment to apply there. In fact, Jamie only had a 10 percent chance of getting into Amherst, and never in my twenty-four years of college advising has anyone with a 10 percent or even a 25 percent chance ever been accepted. He is a wonderful young man, teachers love him, and he has a passion for learning. When he gets a C or B– on an exam or in a semester grade, or a 600 instead of his 700 fantasized critical reading score on the SAT, he gets right up, brushes himself off, and gets on with life. He is more resilient than anyone I have ever met. I love this kid. Everyone does. We all admire him and realize that nothing ever can keep him down. But getting into Amherst? Jamie didn't have a prayer.

It wasn't that he couldn't do the work at Amherst—of course he could, all of the students at a strong high school where 100 percent go on to competitive colleges can do the work everywhere. That's not the point! The point is that colleges are swamped with applicants who are in the acceptable range. Applicants with a strong curriculum, B average, and 680–680 or higher on the SAT amount to a lot of students—and within that range are a lot of terrific kids. It's not "average grades = wonderful kid" vs. "top grades = jerk." It's not a case of whether the college wants the nicest kid in the world with a little less on grades and the SAT vs. great numbers and the most rotten kid in the world. In fact, those rotten kids, jerks, and no-personality kids with the top curriculum, all As, and 800s don't get into Harvard, Princeton, and Stanford either!

So there was Jamie, the optimist, applying early to Amherst without a prayer of getting in. He went merrily along in senior year and told me about each time he went to visit Amherst. He couldn't wait to report that an admissions committee alumna promised to get him introduced to the dean of admissions at a ball game. Just as I knew he would, he got to know Amherst better and better. We all love best what we know best. He handled the deferral in December very well. After all, he just knew he'd get in April, right? Wrong.

What's the danger with this scenario? Jamie never got to know the other colleges on his list. He didn't get into the schools where he had a 50 or 75 percent chance of being accepted. He had only one acceptance—at a school where he had a 90 percent chance of being accepted, and he hadn't even seen that school. Why didn't this great kid make it into the colleges where he had a 75 percent chance of being accepted? Because he "knew" he was getting into Amherst! Why didn't he have other acceptances from the less selective colleges on his list? "Because he showed almost no interest in our college," the other deans reported to me when I queried how they could possibly deny admission to this great kid. His teachers and parents were disappointed that Jamie didn't have more choices, but Jamie had cut off the possibility of other choices by being obsessed with one college.

It's important to keep searching and communicating with all the colleges on your list. Don't be tempted to fixate on just one. It feels very different in April to receive word about the college admissions decisions than you think it will in the fall when you are applying. And it feels really good to have several April choices.

The Kid Behind the Numbers

Right after the numbers, the dean looks at character. College admissions deans look for the strength of a person. A student's integrity and maturity are judged by her activities, interests, and aspirations. Character and personality are not as easy to measure as the numbers in the academic arena. The measure that many deans find most important is how you spend your time when you are not in the classroom and when you are not studying for the classroom. Deans don't ask about sports only to find out whether they can use you on their team; they ask to find out what is important to you. When you have a choice to make about how to spend the next hour, the weekend, your spring break, or your summer, what do you choose?

The admissions deans ask questions that will elicit answers that reveal the character of their applicants. Most deans of admissions are after the same data; we know a lot about how things work at selective colleges because there are so many college application questions out there to read. Some college applications are more fun than others. Sometimes they will ask for you to give your favorite word, time of day, newspaper section—little everyday things that fascinate experienced deans who have read thousands of applications from seventeen-year-old students. If your applications don't have interesting questions, then you can be brave and give fun answers! They'll wake up and smile as they read your application.

▶ ▶ ▶ **THE DEANS ARE** *always looking for the "you" behind the numbers.*

The deans are always looking for the "you" behind the numbers, and if you trust yourself enough, you can really have fun with this kind of section. Of course if you trust yourself enough, you can have fun with the whole process. One of the conditions for trusting yourself is remembering that you don't *have* to get into a particular college. When you can be you and look with curiosity at many possible colleges all over the United States, then you don't feel that pressure of "Is this the right answer? Is this what they are after? Will the dean prefer this or that?" Trying to outguess what a dean will like turns the process into a nightmare and prevents you from being you. Having fun finding ways to express the "you" that your family and friends find so endearing is your task. When colleges ask about your activities, interests, and aspirations, the intent behind the question is this: They want to know how this teenager distinguishes himself when he has a choice in how he will spend his time.

Activities, Interests, and Aspirations

The colleges want to know who you are. They will go into depth about asking you how you spend your time. They may ask questions like these: In which activities are you involved? What form does your involvement take? How many high school years have you been involved in this activity/these activities? How many hours a week do you participate in this activity/these activities? When you are not in the classroom, what are you doing? The college deans will give you a rating for your activities. Try out a few of the questions listed here to get a feel for answering this type of question:

➢ What activities do I enjoy most outside of the classroom?

➢ What do I give up in order to do this activity?

➢ Will there be time and opportunity in college for this activity?

➢ What do my parents expect of me?

➢ What do my friends expect of me?

➢ Who has influenced me the most?

➢ What kinds of surroundings are essential to my well-being?

Many of your parents get off base, way out in left field when it comes to activities. They ask guidance counselors and college deans, "What is the best activity to get into Washington U? What should she do in the summer to get into Bryn Mawr? Is baseball or lacrosse better to get into Tufts?" The point I want you to know is that the college wants to know who you are. Authentic you. What do you like best—baseball or lacrosse? What do you want to do in the summer? It's what you learn from what you do and how you express it in writing that counts most for getting into college. Cutting grass, being a mother's helper, pumping gas all count!

▶▶▶ **IT'S NOT WHAT** *you do in the summer that counts; it's what you learn from what you do. Start!*

When Sally came in to tell me that she won the award in community service in her junior year and she was sure that would give her an edge, I had to tell her that girls are big into community service and it does not always distinguish them in the college selection process. Now if she had a start-up computer business to tell me about, that would be a different story because those young entrepreneurs so seldom are women. If the guys come in with the community service award, that's another story too. So gender makes a difference in the activity.

When you distinguish yourself, be aware of gender stereotypes. Suppose you are a young woman applying to Bowdoin, Colby, and Vassar, where there are about six times as many women applying as young men. If your activity is community service, and your interests are foreign language, humanities, and English, then you have no edge at all—that's what the applications of the majority of young women look like; that's the profile. If your brother has the same record and applies to those colleges, his percent chance to get in will skyrocket! Your chances of getting in will skyrocket too if you spent your summers making a lot of money in some business that you initiated, love physics, and can't wait to take advanced mathematics.

When you tell the college that you went to Chile or Nepal to do community service, they read that as "privileged." The summer programs at Harvard and Wellesley are not connected to the admissions office of the undergraduate colleges! Again, if you go to expensive summer programs, the first message to the colleges is that you can afford them. A parent once asked an Ivy dean of admissions which activities would be most helpful in getting her son into Ivy—going to Harvard summer school, doing community service work in Honduras, or teaching English in China? The dean responded that the son should "pump gas." It's not what you do in the summer that counts; it's what you *learn* from what you do.

Personality, Character, and Relationships to Others

There isn't any part of the college selection process that the deans of admissions haven't thought through. They want to know your personality, your character, and how you get along with others. Harvard's Dean William R. Fitzsimmons is the first to say, "We look at everything. Everything." After all, you are asking to be invited to live in their community. Another Ivy League dean believes that most teenagers nowadays haven't yet had many tests of character. He judges their maturity and integrity by the school letters of recommendation, what the student does in the summer, and in what kinds of community service the student has been involved.

If you only listen to the media and SAT tutors about the "numbers," it may be hard to believe that what you do during your summers matters at all. Here's a true story that will help. A top student from a competitive prep school with 750+ on more than five of her SAT Subject Tests was turned down by Penn on the basis of her lack of interest in others. It's not that community service is the major criterion, but the lack of it can imply such self-interest that the college simply doesn't want such an egocentric person in their community, even if that centeredness is on mathematics and chemistry. So look at your application first for establishing your student worth based on your curriculum, grades, and test scores. Then realize that the rest of the application is set up to seek out clues as to your character, your belief system, your priorities—and nothing demonstrates your values more than how and with whom you spend your time. Think about a college from the perspective of matching who you are with their campus culture.

➢ What adjectives do I use to describe myself?

➢ How would my best friend describe me?

➢ Which relationships are most important to me? Why?

➢ How free do I feel to make my own decisions?

➢ How free do I feel to stand alone among my friends with a point of view different from theirs?

➢ How do I feel about going to a college where the other students are quite different from me?

➢ How do I feel about going to a college very different from my high school?

Many students aren't aware of what they are used to in their own environment because they haven't been asked to consider it. If they live in New York City and go to a small private school, they will often say, "I don't want a college that is too big after going to a small school all my life."

Being from Vermont, I usually respond, "If a New Yorker can't handle 'big', who can?" There is a lot more to your environment than the size of your school. Look around you. What are you used to? How do you get to school? What is your experience with diversity in terms of race and economics? What is your neighborhood like? If you live in a suburb, your high school of two thousand is bigger than most liberal arts colleges. Are you looking for playing it safe or going after adventure? Are you a risk taker, or would you rather watch others go up on those high ropes? Knowing your own values can help you choose the college culture that is best for you.

Think about the campus where you have spent the last three or four years. How diverse is your high school? How diverse are your friends, your community? Many colleges ask students to write an essay about the community in which they grew up. They want to know, among other things, how diversity (or the lack of it) in your community has influenced you.

What does diversity mean anyway? Why is it so important, and why are America's top colleges fiercely competing for the diversity offered by underrepresented groups? First of all, education is following the global economic market and global communicating technology. Educators strongly believe that students learn from each other. Therefore, the more diverse the college community, the more students will learn that diversity is the very foundation of today's age of globalization. You should know too that diversity means much more than the well-publicized racial and ethnic diversity. Diversity to the deans of admissions means all of the underrepresented groups in the world. These groups include first-generation college students; seniors from high schools not yet represented at their college; religious, geographical, and international diversity as well as racial and ethnic.

Just as the economic markets jump from country to country around the world, the American college dean recruits a student from here, another from there—rich and poor, high tech and low tech, from the Far East to the Southern Hemisphere, from Fairbanks to Auckland. From China and Vietnam. American students have to look at the other side of the diversity issue as well. Let's say it out loud: If diversity is in, privilege is out. Think about it: When the deans are searching the globe for the new and exciting, the privileged old tried and true has to be on its way out.

> ▶ ▶ ▶ **EDUCATORS STRONGLY BELIEVE** *that students learn from each other. Therefore, the more diverse the college community, the more students will learn that diversity is the very foundation of today's age of globalization.*

This change has probably been going on for the past twenty years, but it has been only recently that I've noticed myself saying to our seniors, "Don't write your college essay on your summer in Africa, in China, in South America. It just sends up a 'privilege flag', and college deans hate privilege!" That's a strong message from the competitive colleges. It's a lesson that college advisors from the private schools from St. Paul's in New Hampshire to San Francisco University High School to The Lovett School in Atlanta have learned well. We have to take this lesson very seriously when we hear Tom Parker, the dean of admissions at Amherst, tell the parents of New York City's private school students that, in his mind, he deducts one hundred points from their SATs because they all have the advantage of so much SAT tutoring. Now that's an admissions dean's perception of privilege!

▶▶▶ **COLLEGE ADMISSIONS IS** *big business in America today.*

Ronnie Turner, dean of admissions at Washington University, said to me that if the best schools of New York City could see the talents and achievements of Washington University's applicant pool from all over the world, we would realize that only the top quarter of New York's best students could stand up to the competition. And that's not Ivy or the Northeast or West Coast—that's Washington University in St. Louis, Missouri! As anxious as they are, many East and West Coast parents of college applicants don't even have a clue about that level of college admissions competition. Privilege from the strongest education program and private school legacy are no longer the qualities that the colleges value most. Diversity is.

Add to the diversity issue the facts that (a) college applications are increasing each year, (b) the number of competitive colleges where the parents think their children "have" to go is static, and (c) the number of freshman in these colleges remains the same. It's easy to see that traditional, private school names no longer bring promises of Ivy admissions. Personalizing your applications becomes more important each year as thousands of talented and fascinating students from all over the world flock to America's higher education programs.

College admissions is big business in America today. What's big business in America? How about a $3 billion-a-year college admissions business? The American higher education industry is one of our few exports with very little competition. And big business attracts attention. The media has jumped in and adds to the fear of your parents as they read so often about the so-called tight college market and high-testing, full-paying Chinese students flooding our colleges, about SAT coaching at $300 to $900 an hour, and private consultants at $3,000 a shot or $75,000 and more for the "platinum package." Big business is visible to the media when they see the numbers of bookshelves devoted to the college selection process in the bookstores, not to mention the profits at *U.S. News and World Report* from their rankings enterprise. This is not new. We are talking about twenty-five years of big profits—money made from parents' anxiety and fears for their children as they begin the college admissions process.

As diversity, globalization, and the media take over, the college market appears tighter and the college admissions process becomes more enterprising. You've got your work cut out for you on the diversity and international issue. If you are one of the underrepresented groups—black, Hispanic, or American Indian—be sure and acknowledge that diversity on your application. If you are one of the overrepresented groups—white or Asian, and women in most of the applicant pools—then start describing your diversity in other ways. Your primary responsibility is to describe your diversity in how you think, your style, interests, creativity, literary background, and leadership, rather than being labeled as overrepresented or privileged because you are from an excellent high school.

> ▶▶▶ **YOUR PRIMARY RESPONSIBILITY** *is to describe your diversity in how you think, your style, interests, creativity, literary background, and leadership.*

Think about how you will document your diversity, special characteristics, and skills that you will bring to the college to which you are applying. Here is an exercise that helps you to assess yourself for the kinds of personal activities that you have developed throughout high school.

STUDENT SELF-ASSESSMENT

Here are 12 characteristics, interests, achievements, and skills American colleges are looking for. Where do you fit in? Read the following 12 student characteristics. Check the three personal interests that sound most like you. Support your choices by writing a line or two to document them. For example:

1. Leadership:

Vice president of my high school class, team leader of my French club, captain of my soccer team.

2. World view:

Watch international news on TV and online. Occasionally read the *New York Times* and *Wall Street Journal*. Have traveled abroad with my family. Sometimes read the *Economist*. Read international newspapers in my foreign language classes.

3. Public speaker:

Won debate club competition. Have run for office in sophomore and junior class elections which requires several school speeches and taking part on panel discussions.

Check any three of the following 12 interests and write two or three lines to provide evidence of your choices, why you selected these activities, and what you learned from the experience.

1. Leadership:

_____
_____

2. World view:

_____
_____

3. Public speaker:

_____
_____

4. Essay writer:

_____
_____

SELF-ASSESSMENT

5. Science interest and awards:

_____

_____

6. Entrepreneurial (business interests):

_____

_____

7. Intellectual curiosity (reads a lot, asks a lot of questions):

_____

_____

8. Performing arts (document participation and awards in music, theatre, dance):

_____

_____

9. Community service:

_____

_____

10. Organic gardening and nutrition experience:

_____

_____

11. Changing the world experience and interests (climate change, human rights):

_____

_____

12. Sports interest and achievement:

_____

_____

13. Can't find THREE Interests? Add your own personal interests and document with two or three lines:

_____

_____

Who Are the Colleges Looking for?
The Colleges Want to Know

What does "Who are you?" mean to you? That's what the college deans want to know. It means more than your name. More than your test scores. In order to answer that question, start by thinking about what activities you like best, how you spend your free time, and what you learn from your activities about who you are and what kind of a person you are becoming. Look at all of your time: at home, at school, and time away from school and home.

Think about where you spend your time outside of school, and think about your goals and values. Think beyond what your teachers and best friends think about you as a student. Think about the questions below and add some of your own.

> ➢ What kind of person am I?

> ➢ What aspects of my life have I enjoyed the most?

> ➢ What parts do I like the least?

> ➢ How do I define success?

The American college admissions deans are looking for your assessment of yourself. They read your application to find your strength of character. Most deans measure your character by how you spend your time when you are not in the classroom and when you are not studying. They measure character, interests, and your aspirations by your activities. Deans don't ask about sports or the arts only to find out if they can use you on their team or in their bands and orchestras; they ask you to find out what is important to you. When you have a choice to make about how to spend the next hour, the weekend, your spring break, or your summer, what do you choose? The admissions deans ask questions to learn your character from your applications. Understanding how you choose to spend your time when you have free time is the best way to understand who you are, what you value, and what is most important to you. Think about it.

When you write your college applications, you will be asked who you are in many ways. The colleges want to know what kind of person is going to fit best in their college community, what kind of person is going to discuss and debate issues in the classroom, and what kind of person is going to play on the sports teams and in the orchestra. What kind of person is going to be a student leader and contribute most to the everyday life of the college? Think about it. Here's the best question to get started to describe yourself: What do you choose to do when you have a free afternoon or evening?

CHAPTER 2

COLLEGE ADMISSIONS TESTING

Oh no—SATs! "Will a 1500 SAT or ACT 35 get me into Harvard? Yale? Cal Tech? I have to go to Brown or Berkeley or Boston College. When should I take a course to raise my SAT scores?" I say to anyone with a 680 SAT critical reading and a 680 math score or a 29 ACT, and an 85 TOEFL, "No, your test scores will not get you into Williams or the University of Texas; but most important, those scores won't keep you out. And that's all you need to know about SAT and ACT scores. That's all you need to worry about. Don't waste your time and resources worrying about perfect testing, when there are so many interesting and exciting learning experiences in which to invest your energy!" Whatever your scores are, you can be sure that a lot more than SAT or ACT scores goes into the decision the colleges make about you.

You didn't test as high as you thought you would? You heard there is a long list of test optional colleges? Think before you decide against taking SAT/ACTs. Isn't there at least one on your college list that you know would be a great fit for you? If the college says, "test optional," how do you think they decide if you can do the work at their college or not? The crucial question in your mind has to be, what are the colleges looking for in their accepted students? The answer is they are looking for everything: academic rigor – enough to do the work at their particular college. Whether you choose to take college admissions testing or not, all colleges measure your ability to do their academic work. Here's how they do it: 1. The rigor of your curriculum for four years of high school. 2. The grades you received in that curriculum. 3. And lastly, your test scores to support your grades (if you have them). Rigor of curriculum and grades will be the measure of your academic level if you do not have scores. Without a global standard of measure, as SATs/ACTs provide, the college will ask your school more questions about their grading system, more questions about the competition you had in your particular classes. In other words, it is not "easier" to get in without test scores, it is a matter of using other measures to assure colleges where you fit into the particular college's academic standards.

Is there anything about the college selection process that makes you more anxious than taking, receiving, and sending your testing scores to the colleges? The worst part about this anxiety is that it's useless. Most of you have learned this fear through all the test prep companies and tutors, private college consultants, and media that are making a lot of money on your fears. They lead you to think that if you only had twenty or thirty more points on an SAT, you would certainly get into those very selective colleges that you are aiming for. In reality, test scores always disappoint. Remember that half of those 1600 SAT and 99 ACT whizzes don't get into Princeton and Stanford—because there is no score that gets you in. A better way to think about your scores is what will keep you out. If you have a 1350 or 29, you will not be kept out of any college in America because of your test scores.

Let's take the bull by the horns right now and talk about SAT or ACT prep. When you think about it, the numbers craze on SAT and ACT scores—in the media and in your mind—is surpassed only by the way people talk about their weight. It's as if *you* are your test scores. Within this moneymaking test prep machinery, numbers are easy to understand and to sell. And SAT and ACT numbers have been a best-seller in the media for so long, that it's easy to believe the message.

It may be easier to understand the relevance of numbers if we think of height and weight in athletics, instead of SAT scores. For example, we can all agree that an athlete's height enters into the performance of a basketball player. Likewise, weight can be beneficial to the performance of a linebacker. But that's not enough to make an athlete successful in either sport. Most of us easily understand that the numbers, seven feet tall or 275 pounds, hardly predict a winner! And even though the speed of a tennis player's serve can bring her into the top competition, most of us cannot imagine choosing the U.S. Open champion by her hundred-mile-per-hour serve. We all know it's the personality and character behind those stats that makes a champion: motivation, coachability, discipline, and attitude. SAT numbers are the same way. Test numbers are not *you*, and the deans of admissions are after the real you—the fascinating seventeen-year-old student with great character and potential for learning—behind those test numbers.

SAT or ACT?

Here's what high school college counselors have learned about test prep and the differences for students in taking the SAT or the ACT:

1. If a student has taken practice tests, taken both the SAT and ACT, or looked them over and likes one better than the other... go with her feelings. Liking one better than the other gives added confidence to the test-taker. Confidence level in the particular test makes a difference in scores.

2. Studying for both the SAT and the ACT is a waste of time and money. Taking both tests can cause more confusion on test strategies than raise test scores.

3. The SAT rewards thoughtfulness, deliberation, and working through the answers. It contains more heavy reading and historic reading passages.

4. The ACT awards answering surface questions quickly and contains less vocabulary to understand. Risk-taking speed helps toward high scores on the ACT.

When to Take the Tests?

1. Students taking Algebra 2 or Geometry who are not strong readers should wait until May or June of junior year to take the first SAT or ACT and should take the second one in fall of the senior year.

2. Juniors with advanced math and strong readers who have covered history and literature from the 1800s should plan to take the test twice in junior year and possibly once in fall of senior year.

SAT Prep

Numerous studies to measure the effect of coaching on SAT performance have been conducted. There are varying conclusions derived from those studies, but virtually all of them indicate that becoming familiar with the test and developing thinking skills through a secondary school curriculum are the means of achieving significant improvement on ACT and SAT scores. Once you receive your PSAT scores, you often wonder if and when you should consider special review work before taking the SAT. Such work can take the form of individual commitment to building vocabulary and taking practice exams diligently in one of the many review books on the market. Some students choose to work with a private tutor or with a test review program. No matter what method is chosen, many of my students have seen score increases once they have made a commitment to take such work seriously. There are never any guarantees since test taking is not an area where miracles occur, but if you feel anxious, know that you are being prepared for SATs every day in your rigorous high school curriculum as well as in your daily reading of the *New York Times*. The plan that is best for you depends on your history as a test taker, what scores you have now, and your own level of confidence in testing. Prepare yourself for the SATs as you would for sports: Get in shape physically, intellectually, and emotionally!

There are some rules of logic to follow right before and during the exam. We know that college testing is stressful. Cramming the night before does not help. Instead of overwhelming your brain, get a good night's sleep. Be sure to eat a normal breakfast—a meal that is larger than you usually eat can make you sleepy because your body isn't used to digesting so much food. Students with the highest test scores concentrate best for the full three hours. Others "get sick of the test," slow down, and often give up. Look at the clock. Take each question as it comes and give it your best shot. The easy answers count as much as the hard ones. When you go into the third hour, eat some raisins or candy that you've brought with you. Psyche yourself up, tell yourself you are just as fresh this third hour as you were when you walked in. You're young: Three hours of concentration is easy at sixteen and seventeen! Chances are that you won't be devastated with some horrible score. In fact, SAT scores are almost always consistent with your grades at school. And remember that long-term grades count for more than one ACT or SAT exam that only shows what you can do in three hours.

For many of you, college admissions testing often began in freshman year when you took the June SAT Subject Test in biology. About 750,000 of you took the Preliminary SAT (PSAT) in October of your sophomore year, which is for most of you, the first major college admissions test that you took or will take. Sophomores headed for the most selective colleges have also taken the chemistry and math SAT Subject Tests. Juniors will all take the PSAT.

Preliminary SAT (PSAT)

The PSAT is a short version of the SAT: Reasoning Test. About 3.5 million students take the PSAT in grades 10 and 11. It is used to determine U.S. National Merit Scholars in their junior year. It measures verbal reasoning, critical reading, and math problem solving skills that you have developed over many years, both in and out of school. You won't have to recall facts from literature, history, or science. You won't have to define or use grammatical terms. You won't have to write an essay. And you won't need to furnish math formulas; in fact, some formulas will be given on the test for reference. Sophomores take it for practice, but juniors take it to qualify (usually among the top 4 percent in your state) for the National Merit Scholarship Program. The PSAT recognizes outstanding black and Hispanic students as well.

If you are a learning disabled student, accommodations such as extended time, special forms, and verbal proctoring of the test are available if you qualify. Check out your questions with your guidance counselor or the College Board Web site. If you are an American studying abroad or an international school student who wants to get an idea of the American testing system, the PSAT is given in most American and international schools. Contact the College Board through their Web site (www.collegeboard.com) to find the testing site closest to you.

The SAT and ACT Tests

The SAT is a three-hour test that measures critical reading, writing, and mathematical reasoning abilities. The critical reading section tests your ability to analyze reading passages, sentence structures, and connections between pairs of words. The mathematical section tests your abilities in arithmetic, algebra, and geometry. The SAT Subject Tests are one-hour tests in specific subjects. Subject tests measure your knowledge of particular subjects such as English literature, foreign languages, mathematics, science, and history. You should choose which SAT Subject Tests you will take according to the strengths of your academic courses.

The ACT, administered through the American College Testing Program, differs very little from the SAT. A small difference is that the ACT is all multiple choice, while the SAT has "student-produced responses" in the mathematics section.

Some families and coaches think that students do better on the ACT because the numbers are higher on the ACT. Other students have liked the ACT better because the SAT had a stronger emphasis on vocabulary while the ACT focuses on grammar and punctuation. Of course the SAT tutors like both exams and often encourage you to take both because they can make a lot more money if you do. What you should know is that it is also a matter of geography. Let's all remember that a few points on any test does not determine the college decision. Whichever test your high school recommends is probably the one that you will take.

Registering for the SAT and ACT

Most students download the registration forms found on the ACT or College Board Web site at www.ACTstudent.org or www.college-board.com. You can also pick up the necessary registration forms for your SAT, ACT, and SAT Subject Tests in your guidance counselor's office. You will need your high school CEEB code number for the SATs. Be sure to use the exact same name each time you register for a College Board test. The College Board's computer system will send all your tests together, but only if you write your name and address exactly the same each time.

Score Choice! Superscore!! SuperSATs!!! Power Scores!!!!

College admissions is big business in America. College admissions testing takes a big cut of those profits. Score Choice: Confusing? You bet it is! Here's the truth of the matter:

You have a choice to send the colleges your top SAT scores from several testing dates. You also have a choice to send your top scores from individual SAT Subject Tests taken on different dates. There is also a choice to send the top scores from one date. Those choices encourage the test-prep companies to advise you to take the SATs and Subject Tests several times to get your top scores. It also encourages you to feel as if you are in control of your SAT scores. What's the catch?

The colleges decide which you can send. For example, you can send top scores from one test date, but then there are options 1 and 2. Or you can send top SAT Subject Test scores from one test date. Again, there is a Version 1 and 2 within that choice. Different colleges permit different options. You must send what the particular colleges require.

What to do? Send them all! Don't waste your time trying to guess which combination is best for what school. If University of Chicago wants only the top scores, they will choose only top scores; if Notre Dame wants just the top section, Version 2, that's what they will take from your SAT scores and write in only those scores on your application file. If Bowdoin wants to see all of your test scores, they will require all of your scores. All of those choices together are called: Score Choice. Throughout your agony on deciding what to do, remember this, SATs do not get you in! Once you have the numbers that document that you can do the work, the admissions dean goes right on to the question, "Who is this kid behind those numbers?" Reading your transcript, application, essay, and how you present yourself in writing are where you should be spending your time.

Take a look and see for yourself who wants what. Here is the College Board link to what each college requires:

http://professionals.collegeboard.com/profdownload/sat-score-use-practices-list.pdf

Last word of advice: Send them all!

Test Centers

Many of your high schools will not be an SAT or ACT test site, so you will need to register to take your tests elsewhere. The registration bulletins provide a list of possible test sites for your state. Look for the most convenient sites; you will be asked to list two choices. The earlier you register, the better chance you have to take your SATs in your choice of sites. Check out the dates and deadlines as soon as you know which tests you have to take.

Juniors, you probably won't take any SATs until May of your junior year, and your SAT Subject Tests should always be taken in June at the end of your coursework. Usually the deadline for registration is about one month ahead of the test date. For example, if the SAT test date is May 5, the international deadline (that is, for international students and Americans abroad) will be March 27, and the deadline for students in the United States will be March 29.

Fee Waivers

Fee waivers are available for students who cannot afford to take the college entrance exams. Your guidance office has the fee waivers and the guidelines for using them. Do not hesitate to ask for a waiver! Many counselors are far too busy to inform you of the fee waivers, but they do exist. Ask for information regarding waivers for college applications and specifically for the PROFILE, which is a part of the College Board's College Scholarship Service (CSS). Check with your counselor for the proper forms before you register for SATs or ACTs.

Nonstandard Testing

Nonstandard testing is helpful to those who have a diagnosed and properly documented learning disability or physical handicap. ETS offers extended time, large print, and other accommodations for those who qualify. Talk with your guidance counselor to learn more about this testing option.

When to Take the SAT

Juniors will take the SAT or ACT in May. Everyone will give you different advice on when to take your SATs. Let's remember that you are, like a scientist, learning to collect the data before making a decision. Always be aware of where the advice is coming from. If your SAT tutor says to take the ACT and the SAT in your sophomore year, or January or March of your junior year, just realize what's in it for them for you to take the tests often. Some of your families may think it makes sense to take the SAT during spring break when you aren't as pressured with schoolwork and finals. Just know that the research shows that the longer you are in school, the harder you are working, the more those little gray cells are putting in overtime, and the better your test results will be. Believe it or not, your vacation is not the best time to take the SAT, even though it may first appear that way.

Many seniors take the SAT a second time in the fall or winter of their senior year, depending on their junior scores. The colleges will look at your test scores as late as March of senior year when making their decisions (but you won't be winning the dean's heart by not having your tests there when they are ready to look at them). December of your senior year should be your latest date for taking college tests (although there are always exceptions to everything you are going to do in this process).

When to Take the SAT Subject Tests

SAT Subject Tests are taken in June of any high school year. Biology students in ninth and tenth grades are usually the first to take the SAT Subject Tests. A student takes the SAT Subject Test whenever a course such as biology or chemistry is completed after ninth and tenth grades. Some math students take the Math Level I test as soon as they have completed Algebra II and geometry. Most selective colleges require two SAT Subject Tests in addition to the SAT. Juniors usually take mathematics, foreign language, science and a third test on history or another foreign language or science. Doesn't that make sense? Now listen to a story, one of many "misguided advice" stories that I hear all too often.

Last summer a rising senior came to my office to discuss colleges with me. After talking a while about what she was looking for in a college, I commented, "With those grades in that tough curriculum, and those super SATs, you must have killed those SAT Subject Tests!"

"I didn't take them," she answered.

"You didn't take them? Didn't you say that you took honors biology in junior year?

"Yes."

"And you didn't take the SAT Subject Test when you finished the course?"

"No, my guidance counselor said to wait for senior year to take our SATs."

"Does that make sense to you?"

"No."

The moral of this story is that no matter where the advice comes from, it must make sense to you! If you want to go to a selective college, take the SAT Subject Tests in June of the year when you finish the course—it's a given. I don't care if it's Prince Harry who is giving you advice or the nicest guidance counselor in the whole wide world, if it doesn't make sense to you, ask again or ask someone else.

Seniors will take SAT Subject Tests in December only if they need a third test or want to try for higher scores. There are eighteen different subject tests, and they are content oriented. They measure how much math, English, physics, French, or U.S. history you know. Because they are subject oriented, these are tests that can and should be studied for. Each test lasts one hour; you may take up to three on any test day. Many colleges require at least one of the two math tests. Others require particular tests, and still others require none for admission. It is up to you to check out what each college on your list requires.

How do you know which Subject Tests to take? Always take the math. If you are in doubt about which level of math or which second subject to take, discuss your testing options with your teachers and guidance counselor. Your best bet is to consider your grades in the subject, your teacher's recommendation, and how well you do on a practice test. These factors will help you make a sound decision. You will find a practice test for every SAT Subject Test in a free booklet from the College Board called *Taking the SAT Subject Test*. Ask your guidance counselor for a copy.

How Many SAT Subject Tests Do the Colleges Require?

Every college is different in their test requirements, so make sure that you check online or with the college rep to get the official word about required testing. Harvard and Princeton require three SAT Subject Tests, but Williams, Pomona, Yale and most of the other highly selective colleges require two Subject Tests. "What do the colleges require?" is the wrong question. The right question is, "How many courses of my high school achievement can I document through the SAT Subject Tests?"

You are in high school to build as strong an academic record as you can. At the end of every science course, foreign language sequence, history and English course, take the Subject Test. The more and varied academic areas you can document by nationally tested strengths, the stronger record you can show the colleges. The top students for the most competitive colleges will submit six or more Subject Test scores over the course of four years. With Score Choice in place, there is no down side to taking the Subject Tests. If you don't do well in the physics Subject Test, then use the biology results. The point to be made here is that you are taking these exams for you—it's your record, and you want it to represent you in the best way that is possible. Don't even ask the colleges what they require because you are not looking for minimum requirements to get in to college—you are looking at how well you can document your achievement on a national level. You are going to say to yourself, "Let me document my academics from freshman year through first semester senior year, do my best, and then see which colleges are interested in me with this record." Period.

Score Reports to Colleges

At the time you register for the SATs or ACTs, you will have an opportunity to list four colleges (by code number) to which you can have your scores sent without additional fees. There is a charge for sending scores to each college after the first four. You, not your high school, are responsible for sending your official SAT or ACT scores to your colleges. All your SAT scores go to the colleges unless you opt for Score Choice (explained earlier). Most colleges use your highest scores. You should be aware that they usually look at the highest critical reading and the highest math, not necessarily the highest *set* resulting from an individual testing date. SAT scores are mailed directly to your home and high school about three weeks after the test is taken. Scores will also be mailed to the colleges that you designated when you registered for the test.

NOW HEAR THIS! **Students** must request that the Education Testing Service (ETS) officially send their ACT or SAT scores to the colleges. The scores on your transcript are not official. Your college application will not be complete until the college receives your ACT or SAT scores directly from ETS or ACT. (Seniors, does it sound like I'm making way too much of this little point? If you only knew how many seniors think that if it's on their transcript, they don't have to send it. Woe is me trying to get that second point across—you know the first point, right? Here it is again: SAT Subject Tests in June after you finish a course, no matter what.)

Optional SATs and ACTs

Some admissions deans of colleges and universities are so disgusted with the $3 billion industry that has grown around SAT and ACT tutoring that they elected to make the SAT optional rather than required. Likewise, officials for a few large state universities decided they would have more applicants if they created an optional test choice. Over a thousand colleges have become test optional in the past four years. Some of those same colleges still require SAT Subject Tests though, and chances are that of the current seventy five or so colleges that do not require SATs, at least one college on *your* list will require them. So don't even think of not taking them! That means that even if Bowdoin and Wesleyan have an optional SAT, you probably have Carleton or Claremont McKenna, and a couple more on your list that do require it.

So take the SAT or ACT. Decide after you get the results if you are going to send them to the optional test colleges. The advice I give my students is that if you have at least a 550–550–550, send them. You don't want the deans of admissions to assume that your scores are much lower than a 550 and that this is your rationale for withholding them. If you are one of the very few students whose top grades in a rigorous curriculum and SAT Subject Tests are a hundred points above your SATs, then this option is designed for you! Here are some of the current list of colleges that have the SAT option, and it's growing: Bard, Bates, Bowdoin, University of the Holy Cross, Connecticut College, Denison, Dickinson, Franklin and Marshall, Gettysburg, Guilford, Hamilton, Hampshire, Hartwick, Hobart and William Smith, Lake Forest, Lawrence, Lewis and Clark, Middlebury, Mount Holyoke, Muhlenberg, Pitzer, Rollins, St. John's College (MD and NM), Saint Lawrence, Sarah Lawrence, Union, Ursinus, Wheaton (MA), and Worcester Polytechnic Institute. Test optional universities include the University of Chicago, George Washington University, and University of Texas (Austin).

Check the testing requirements for each of your colleges to be sure you comply. Colleges are different and many change their testing requirements from year to year. You are responsible for knowing the admissions requirements for every college or university to which you apply. Find the latest test optional colleges online at www.fairtest.org.

Advanced Placement Tests

Advanced Placement (AP) tests are given in May. These tests are designed to measure your mastery of college-level work in specific courses. Even though most students take an AP exam at the end of an AP course, that is, a prescribed curriculum for a college-level course administered by the College Board, students can also take the exam without taking the course. For example, many competitive high schools offer a strong enough curriculum in English and U.S. history that students do well on the AP exams. The point of the exam is to earn college credits. For some students that means saving a year's tuition because they start college with thirty college credits, giving them advanced standing. Students who speak a second language, or if English is their second language, often take an AP test in their other language—Spanish, Russian, Chinese, Hebrew, or whatever their language is—without taking the AP course. As the scores are your own, you don't have to send them to the colleges, and if you have the money for each exam, many of you should go ahead and see how well you do.

AP exams are scored from 1 to 5, a 5 being the highest score. Many students record a 3 and above (or 4 and 5 if applying to the most selective colleges) on their transcript for added documentation of their academic achievement. Senior scores on these tests have no impact on the college admissions process because the test is given after all admissions decisions have been made. Enrolling and doing well in an AP course, however, will show up on your transcript, and a junior AP score of 4 or 5 is a strong academic credential for your college application. There is nothing that helps more in the admissions decision than doing well in AP or International Baccalaureate (IB) courses, which are by definition the most rigorous offered at your high school. But remember—the key words here are "doing well."

Taking APs for how they will look on your transcript is not a sound principle for curriculum decisions. Many students are crying their eyes out in October of their senior year over the impossible AP calculus or AP biology course. Or they begged to get into AP European history because they wanted an AP on their transcript but are now getting a C– or D in the work. Qualifying for one course isn't the only question at hand; the balance of your whole course load also must be considered. Of course you could do an AP or two if that's all you had to do, but how likely is that? You have a lot more on your plate, right? Listen to your teacher recommendations before you sign up for APs. Look at your exam score in the last course, not just the final grade, which also reflects homework and discussion or participation grades. And never base a decision on how it looks to others.

International Baccalaureate and A-Level Examinations (IB)

Students will take IB and A-Level exams only in schools that offer an IB or A-Level curriculum. Many students and parents ask, "Which do the U.S. colleges like best, the IB, A-Level, or AP programs and exams?" The answer is that colleges like whatever you do and learn from! They want to know if you are taking the most rigorous curriculum offered at your high school. They don't care if those courses are called by the names AP, IB, A-Level, Honors, or simply described as the most rigorous courses on the school profile. There is no "best" curriculum name; the best one is the most competitive course load as described by your school officials.

CHAPTER 3

WHAT'S OUT THERE? RESEARCHING THE COLLEGES

How can you learn about all of America's colleges? How do you find the best match—the best college for you? Big or small, paraprofessional or liberal arts, conservative or liberal, private or public, East or West—there are many things to consider. Looking at categories such as size, program offerings, philosophical or religious orientation and location can be helpful, but categories and perceptions can at times be deceiving. In this chapter we'll look at ways to broaden categories and widen perceptions so you can find the best school for you.

Research skills are essential for making a good college decision. That means collecting data from a broad range of sources, looking at the information and weighing it without being judgmental. You want to learn for yourself about the college. It's easy to go on hearsay. ("Someone told me that Williams is too small, someone told me that Michigan is too big, someone told me that UC Santa Barbara is a party school, someone told me that Grinnell is in a cornfield, someone told me that Rice is too hot, that Carleton is too cold, someone told me. . . .")

It's easy to say to your guidance counselor, "Give me my college list." Fortunately for you, good decision-making doesn't work that way. Every college has something for someone. Every college is wonderful for someone. But there is no college that is wonderful for everyone! Knowing you as you know yourself, there are many colleges where you will be happy (you'll fit in with the other students, find the level of education you need and want, be productive, feel good on campus, and more). Researching the colleges means finding several that you'd really like to attend. It doesn't make sense to have colleges on your list just because you can get in if you don't want to go there! You need to create a list of colleges where you do want to go. Of course you will want to go to some colleges more than others, but your research will open your eyes to new possibilities and options.

So, how can you learn about the colleges? To sway a particular college admissions dean, you will have to know that school well enough to explain the reasons you are the good match for that campus culture. You are going to research colleges from a great variety of sources. Most of you will have the opportunity to gather information about schools at college fairs as well as through college guides. You'll meet college representatives at your high school and read catalogs, college homepages on the Internet, as well as books. You will visit campuses and maybe even speak with alumni.

Learn how to trust your own research. When you read or hear something about a college, notice who said it. Was it a representative of the college? What's their bias? Was it a student? What's his bias? Was it a college guide? Who wrote the guide: an educator, a student, an entrepreneur? What's in it for them? Why do they have that particular view of the college? For example, one of my high school seniors came back from a Tulane presentation at a New York City hotel and said, "I'm in love with Tulane; I just have to apply there!" Good for the college rep, he did his job well. His job is to get as many applicants as he can for his college class.

> ▶▶▶ **WHEN YOU READ** *or hear something about a college, notice who said it. What's their bias? Why do they have that particular view of the college?*

You will ask graduates from your high school who go there: how large the freshman classes are, and who teaches freshmen. How accessible are the college's libraries, labs, and computers? Do you have to take math or foreign language to graduate? Is there a core curriculum? Is there a freshman seminar? What are the distribution requirements? You will check out the college guides that will tell you if the college offers military training programs (ROTC)? Is there an internship program? How many freshmen stay for sophomore year (retention rate)? What percentage of the freshmen will graduate? What's the percent of students in sororities and fraternities on this campus?

You've been in science classes, at least two or three with lab work, right? And you've taken social science, history, for example. Our model for learning about the colleges will be as a scientist—a social scientist, an anthropologist to be exact. An anthropologist studies human societies—different cultures, their daily behavior, ceremonies, language, food, families, relationships. All of these things come together and are called ethnography.

▶▶▶ **OUR MODEL FOR** *learning about the colleges will be as a scientist—an anthropologist to be exact. You are going to use the scientific collection of data to learn all that you can about the campus cultures on your final college list.*

You are going to be an ethnographer in the field of anthropology and use the scientific collection of data to learn all that you can about the campus cultures on your final college list. You have learned in science that you don't know the answer before you collect the data. You don't know the conclusion until you've done your lab work. Sometimes you work in teams; sometimes you take field trips. I take my junior class on a field trip to visit three colleges in the Philadelphia area: one large Ivy university, the University of Pennsylvania; one woman's college, Bryn Mawr; and one selective liberal arts college—either Haverford or Swarthmore—depending where we have the most students from our high school that year. They read *The Ultimate Guide to America's Best Colleges* and *The Fiske Guide to Colleges* before they go. They learn to "see" the college campus, the campus culture. My students have already heard the names of these well-known, designer-label colleges. These juniors try to put all of that hearsay aside, as they go from one campus to the other to collect their data. They get a tour, an information session, and lunch with our own high school graduates who are now students on those campuses. You can do the same thing on your own, with your parents and with other seniors in your class. Keep your answers and observations in a notebook—no one can possibly remember the data collected from ten to twenty different campus cultures! And remember that until you collect information from each college on your list, you should not make judgments about any of them. It's from your collected data that you will decide which eight colleges will be at the top of your list.

Research Questions

We start with four research questions: What's it like? Can I get in? How much does it cost? What will become of me?

1. What's it like?

Think about questions that will guide you in collecting the data that you are going to need in order to decide where you are going to apply to college. This is the anthropologist part—the search to help you measure the campus culture. You will look at factors such as size, location, number of students, percent of minority students, geographical percentages, percent of residential students, self-contained campus or not, beauty of campus, types of programs offered, athletic division, and who you know there. You will try to figure out if it's a collegiate campus culture (big sports, fraternities, students talk about sports between classes, big fun—such as Wisconsin, Indiana, Duke, and Northwestern, and preppy such as Middlebury and Colby); or an intellectual campus culture (students talk about books they've read and class discussions between classes and in the dorms—such as Swarthmore, Bard, Grinnell, Chicago, and Pomona); or an artistic campus culture (performing arts majors, more arts outside of class than sports such as conservatories, RISD, SCAD, Skidmore, and Vassar). See below: Can I get in? for special considerations for the arts student. Or perhaps you will explore a preprofessional campus culture (business and management majors such as Babson and Bentley or Wharton, Case Western, or state universities with a college of business); or a research university with students working toward a graduate school admission in law, medicine, or engineering such as Rochester, Rice, Cornell, Penn, and state universities.

To jump start your understanding of what kind of campus culture is the best match for you, take this Ten-Step Quiz: Campus Culture: Find My Match!

Who is this kid behind that GPA and those SAT scores?

The colleges want to know. You want to know!

FIND YOUR MATCH!

Talking to a sophomore at the University of Maryland, the young man explained, "I transferred for the architecture program and they dropped it for financial reasons my first semester." "Why didn't you transfer?" "Because I love it here!" Students leave college because they don't fit in. They stay because it's a great match, the place where they can relax enough to feel confident as they live and learn at their best. Where will you fit in? What's the best campus culture for you? The person you want to be? Take this 10-Step Quiz and find out—choose one for each question.

1. What is your favorite school club or activity?
a. SAT prep group
b. environmental club
c. sports
d. philosophy club
e. music or drama club

2. You're planning Friday night with your friends, do you go to the
a. battle of the bands
b. USA-China exchange student program
c. high school arts festival
d. science fair workshop
e. climate change film

3. What was or is your favorite subject in junior year?
a. art, music, or dance class
b. chemistry or physics

c. social science
d. history
e. English literature

4. What kind of student are you?
a. I like to read and discuss in small study groups everything an author writes
b. I like time and space to try new mediums and designs for my ideas
c. I like to study in the library until I really understand my homework before I relax
d. I like to do my homework and leave plenty of time to work on my community service projects
e. I study my favorite subjects and don't mind winging it once in a while for the rest

5. What's your favorite sport or recreation activity?
a. the gym: treadmill, rowing machine, weights
b. biking, kayaking, camping out
c. team sports: football, basketball, and baseball
d. tennis, swimming, and the gym
e. yoga, dance

6. What do you consider your best quality to highlight on your college application?
a. curiosity
b. imagination
c. work ethic
d. compassion
e. loyalty

7. When you daydream about Saturday night at college, what will you be doing?
a. fund-raising for a water purification group
b. cheering for the home team
c. attending a Dostoyevsky lecture
d. attending the city philharmonic concert
e. attending an event for medical research internships

8. You are filling out your housing form for college. Where will you want to live?
   a. a condo near campus
   b. theme house on campus
   c. fraternity or sorority house
   d. living and learning center
   e. downtown apartment

9. Imagine walking on campus and it begins to snow, what are you talking about?
   a. the ski report for Saturday
   b. the Jean-Paul Sartre film on Saturday
   c. the winter photography show
   d. selling pizzas in the dorms for all of the snow-bounds this weekend
   e. the special needs at the soup kitchen this weekend

10. What kind of friends do you hope to have when you get to college?
    a. innovative friends who like to go to performances and art galleries
    b. serious friends who are in college to get ahead in the world
    c. friends who take action for justice
    d. friends who show up at the games and know how to have a good time
    e. friends who'd rather socialize with a few than party with a crowd

Key

	Red	Purple	Blue	Gold	Green
1	c	d	e	a	b
2	a	b	c	d	e
3	d	e	a	b	c

4	e	a	b	c	d
5	c	d	e	a	b
6	e	a	b	c	d
7	b	c	d	e	a
8	c	d	e	a	b
9	a	b	c	d	e
10	d	e	a	b	c

Circle each letter you chose for all ten questions. Go down each vertical color column, starting with question one through question ten, and give yourself ten points for each letter that you chose. Add them up! Let's say you have 7 red, 2 gold, and 1 blue. That would be 70% Collegiate, 20% Preprofessional, and 10% Creative . Match your scores with the campus culture descriptions below.

College Culture Descriptions

Red = Collegiate campus culture such as University of Texas, Duke, Northwestern, Georgetown, Vanderbilt, or smaller and collegiate such as Colgate, Denison, and Wake Forest. A campus culture where you will find big sports, fraternities, and where you will talk about sports, parties, and friends between classes and in the dorms;

Purple = Intellectual campus culture such as Carleton, Chicago, Grinnell, Pomona, and Swarthmore where you and your friends will spend your time talking about books you've read, where you will continue your discussions from class, argue and debate about academics, politics, and economics;

Blue = Creative campus culture for design and performing arts majors such as conservatories Juilliard and Oberlin or design schools such as Rhode Island School of Design, Savannah School of Arts and Design where you and your friends will talk and sing between classes and in the dorms about the arts, practice sessions, gallery openings, fashion, and upcoming performances;

Gold = Preprofessional campus culture where you and your friends talk between classes and in the dorms about GPAs, MCATs, GREs, LSATs, M.B.A.'s, start-up companies, the global economy, medical and law school, business, engineering, and architecture schools, such as Cornell, UNC, Stanford, Wharton, MIT, Berkeley, University of Illinois, SUNY: Buffalo, and Carnegie Mellon;

Green = Activist campus culture where your friends and you will protest, organize, demonstrate, boycott, and talk about human rights, animal rights, environmental, and climate change issues between classes, in the dorms, and on the quad such as Grinnell, Haverford, Oberlin, Pitzer, and Wesleyan.

How did you do? Are you strongest in Collegiate? Second in Preprofessional? Is an Activist culture important to you? Remember that these categories are determined by what students talk about outside of the classroom. You know, at breakfast, lunch, and dinner. Between classes, in the dorm, the locker room, the student union, at the games, having a coffee, in the library, and everywhere you will go. Campus culture is the heart of student life on campus.

Think about it. Does it make sense? With your best campus cultures match in mind, you are now ready to research the colleges with the most "you" in the campus culture as an important ingredient of how you choose where you will apply to go to college.

2. Can I get in?

You will follow the same sort of process in gathering data for acceptance requirements of the colleges on your list. Perhaps you will ask how selective each college is. You might want to get an idea regarding your competition. Ask such questions as these: Is my record as good or better than most accepted? What is the SAT range of accepted students? Check *Fiske* and *Ultimate* guides for selectivity information (take special note of the selectivity acceptance rates of colleges in the *Ultimate Guide to America's Best Colleges*). What is the admissions track record of graduates from your high school who have applied there in the past three years? Ask your guidance counselor. Don't ask the deans of admissions what SATs are needed to get in—it's the number one question that they hate. Instead, ask the dean about things he loves to talk about, such as questions about the particular academic departments that interest you. For example, you might ask, "What about the music and arts colleges?" You might even have concerns regarding the curriculum. So ask, "Is the freshman course load in a given area of study more demanding than that of other freshmen accepted?"

If you are looking for a professional career in the arts—theatre, music, film, photography, visual arts—then there are special considerations such as the audition, CDs of your work, and portfolios (often accounting for 80% of your chances for getting in). Curriculum, grades, and SATs, even with the top letters of recommendation, can't begin to provide the assessment of students with special talents. Students with extensive musical training who are looking to major in music have two basic categories from which to choose: music conservatories and schools of music at four-year universities. Music conservatories tend to be small (200-900), students major in performance or composition only, the faculty for each instrument often defines the institution, and the student will earn a Bachelor of Music Degree (as opposed to B.A. or B.F.A). The conservatory admission is highly selective according to the opening each year by instrument, the audition is the primary criterion for admission, SATs are usually not required, and scholarships are based on merit rather than on financial need.

University schools of music vary in program complexity according to the size of the college. A great variety of music majors are available such as jazz, sound engineering, musical theatre, and music education. Students study the liberal arts as well as music, and they can have a traditional collegiate experience. Admission to a university school of music is based on both music and academics. A website to help you with your admissions portfolio and much more is found at www.art-schools.com.

3. How much does it cost?

Again, assemble a set of questions designed to find answers to the cost of each college on your list. Here are some examples: If it's a state university in another state, is it worth spending more money on tuition than it would cost to attend my own state university? Does it sound better because it's somewhere else? Are the "public Ivies" (UC Berkeley, UVA, UCLA, Michigan, UNC Chapel Hill, William and Mary, UC San Diego, Wisconsin) a better value than a private college? Do I have a maximum amount I can spend? What are my parents willing to spend? What is the real price? Where can I find out more about financial aid? (Start your research with reading Chapter 6—College Economics 101.)

4. What will become of me?

As a part of your research criteria, you want to include questions that will lead you to understand what doors your college education will—or will not—open for you after graduation. Ask about a school's graduates when the college reps come to your school and at college fairs. It's also a perfect question for the college interview. Most students are so intent on getting in that they never ask what will become of them if they go to a particular college, especially one they can't wait to attend. College deans love this question because it shows a lot of confidence on your part. You've reached a level beyond "Can I get in?"

Here are some questions to get you started as you explore what will become of you after graduation: What do the graduates do? How many go on to graduate school? Which graduate schools do they attend? What kinds of jobs do the students get when they graduate? How many companies recruit on campus? How many graduates go into start-up companies? What percentage of graduates will go to med school, business school, law school, schools of education or into Ph.D. programs? Where do they go and what are their fields of specialization?

Keep Your Eyes—and Options—Open

Big or small, East or West, hot or cold—where in this big country or abroad are you going to begin to look for a college? How far away from home you go depends a lot on your adventurous spirit and your feelings about weather and geography. If you are considering even one university out of your geographical limits, then consider the whole country. If you are considering a college outside of the USA, then consider the world. Look and learn about all the best places that fit the description of the college that you seek. Students will tell me that they want to go to the Northeast, and then they add Emory and Occidental. "But they aren't Northeast," I point out. "I know, but . . ."

If you're from the West and are considering engineering at MIT, then look everywhere! Look at Cornell and RPI in northern New York, Rice in Texas, Columbia in New York City, as well as Swarthmore,

Union, and Brown, which all have engineering schools. There are also Case Western in Ohio and Carnegie Mellon in Pittsburgh. Don't limit your research by categories that may change before you choose your final eight.

If you want to limit the size of the colleges you choose for your top eight, then research college populations; but don't cut your initial possibilities too quickly! Numbers don't always tell the truth. Many juniors come in and say, "I want a medium-sized college, one with around five or six thousand students." Look through the guides and you will see that the majority of American colleges are small liberal arts colleges or big state universities. Stereotypes can be very deceiving. Big schools like Wisconsin, Texas, and UNC at Chapel Hill students are more than numbers. The students on those campuses relate to each other and to their professors, and quickly break into small manageable friendship groups through living and learning groups and their special interests. A big university soon breaks down into friends from your sports team, music and theater groups, dorm-floor pals, suite-mates, sink-mates, political science class, lab partner or freshman seminar, so that you are not dealing with the whole university at once. The size of your high school has less to do with the ideal size of your college than your personality and what adventures you are ready for. Sure, you may have to take more initiative with that student-to-faculty relationship at a large school, but loads of eighteen-year-olds are ready for that! If a "family" community is important to you, think two thousand students and under. If diversity, high energy, big-time sports, fraternities, both difficult and easy courses, and big-time fun are important to you, think over ten thousand.

If you want to check out colleges by popular majors, you will miss the colleges who send the most students to business, law, and medical schools. The Ivies and most selective colleges don't have majors called pre-med and pre-law. In fact, graduate school deans get sick of reading all of those applications from chemistry and biology majors. They love to see an English major or an art history major who has taken enough chemistry to do well on the MCATs to be a shoo-in for competitive medical school programs, or a Spanish or religion major who takes the LSATs and pops out of a pool of government, political science, or history majors for the best law schools. Besides, choosing a college by major is often misguided; students leave college because they don't fit in, which has nothing to do with ranking or major. Most important, "If the college does a good job with your education," says Ted O'Neill, former Dean of Admissions at the University of Chicago, "you will change your mind three times freshman year about what you want to study!" Let's take a closer look at all of the places you can research to learn more about what's out there.

> ▶▶▶ **A BIG UNIVERSITY** *soon breaks down into friends from your sports team, music and theater groups, dorm-floor pals, suite-mates, sink-mates, political science class, lab partner or freshman seminar, so that you are not dealing with the whole university at once.*

Researching Campus Cultures

You will gather general data from outside the college before you turn to learning more specifics from particular college sources.

College Guides

The bookshelves are lined with college guides. Begin your search with the best:

The Ultimate Guide to America's Best Colleges (SuperCollege, latest edition), Describing more than 300 colleges, this college guide addresses their academics, majors, student life, athletics, student body, distinguished alumni, admissions/financial aid, and postgraduation success. Student quotes from a national survey accompany each description along with an honest appraisal of each college's strengths and weaknesses. Extensive data for each college is provided, including statistics on the student composition, class sizes, most popular majors, admissions rates, required standardized tests, deadlines, college costs, and financial aid. There is expert advice on how to select the right college, complete the strongest college applications, and win the best financial-aid package from the college, as well as rankings of the 100 Best College Values.

The Fiske Guide to Colleges by Edward Fiske (latest edition). If you have money for only one guide, buy *Fiske*. This essay-style guide provides interesting information and evaluations for three hundred plus of the most selective and most interesting undergraduate colleges. It is an educator's view of the college culture and student life on campus. It's the best—read it! Don't take too seriously the ACTs and SATs required to get in, or the rating of the colleges. Only your own guidance counselor will know which SATs, curriculum, and grades are acceptable to a particular college. It's the essay about the campus environment that is important in this guide. You'll start to get an idea of differences in campus cultures as soon as you read about several colleges. It's a great place to get an idea of what's out there while you are collecting data. The three hundred plus colleges in this guide represent the top 10 percent of America's colleges. They are all exceptional, and you'll see that you have a lot to choose from in terms of campus culture and selectivity.

Who is This Kid? Colleges Want to Know! Writing Exercises for Winning Applications, by Joyce Slayton Mitchell (Critical Thinking Co.) Who is this kid? That's what the college deans of admissions want to know. Self-assessment writing exercises, with communications and how to research your choices skills. Students will learn how to separate themselves from the hundreds of other American and international students applying to the same competitive colleges. Ebook also available online from Amazon and www.criticalthinking.com/who-is-this-kid-book.

The College Handbook (The College Board, latest edition). This is one of the most accurate and up-to-date "big" college guides available. The College Board collects the data each year—including which SAT tests are required by each college—from its own membership. Every college in the country is in this guide. *Fiske* and the *Ultimate* guides describe 10 percent of the most selective and interesting colleges in America. Those three hundred plus colleges, along with the other 90 percent of American colleges, will be cited in *The College Handbook*. Be sure to read the Student Life section; check out the percentage of students living in the dorms, the percentage belonging to fraternities, and the athletic division.

LGBTQ (https://www.collegechoice.net/college-resources-for-lgbt -students) Take a look at this website with special considerations for LGBTQ students choosing their college campus culture.

Hillel Guide to Jewish Life. If you are Jewish or have a Jewish heritage and want to find out how to find the best campus culture for Jewish interests, take a look at the Hillel website and college advice:

https://www.hillel.org/college-guide/about-the-college-guide. You may not care; on the other hand, you want to learn if you will be one of a crowd, or if you will be known only as the Jewish kid on campus. The Hillel website also describes the Jewish communities outside colleges that often invite college students to their homes for holidays.

America's top African-American college guidance service, *Black Excel* is one website to start your college search—check out www.blackexcel.org. Also take a look at the latest book for historically black colleges at: https://www.collegechoice.net/rankings/best-historically-black-colleges-universities/

International Student Guide (www.InternationalStudentGuidetothe USA.com) is available in both English and Spanish. This guide helps international students with the wide range of possibilities for study in America from community colleges to graduate schools.

▶ ▶ ▶ **KIDS AREN'T ALIKE** *and don't want the same campus culture—what is supportive for one may not be the best for another.*

If you are questioning your sexuality or identify with the LGBTQ group, you need to know what clues to look for in order to find the most supportive campus culture—or at least learn how you can keep away from the worst. Begin by looking at how this website figures out the best campus cultures for you.

Certainly kids aren't all alike and don't want the same campus culture—what is supportive for one may not be the best for another. Some young women want to go to a women's college where they will get the support as women. And yet, for many reasons, others don't. Some black students want to leave their suburban "white high school" environments and try Spelman, Morehouse, Howard, or another historically black college community for four years—still, other black students insist on integration. Some gay students will want to be in an environment with a strong gay community such as Earlham, Oberlin, Wesleyan, or Yale, while others won't care. For students seeking a gay social life, it's safe to say that the more egalitarian the campus, the more likely they will find it.

When leadership for student government and major activities are controlled by independents as well as by fraternities, the chances increase for an egalitarian environment. You should be very aware that big-time fraternities equal big-time trouble for minorities. Any campus that condones exclusivity in social life and student activities is not a safe place for the excluded. High school students certainly realize that popularity and exclusivity always hurt the outside student.

When a college has a history of admitting young women and blacks, high school students can count on finding a more open and supportive community for *all* minorities. Another idea to consider is the size of the college. The Ivies or state and private universities that are big enough to have large numbers of diverse groups on campus tend to facilitate an environment where students form their own communities.

If you want to apply to a college where you have no idea about the campus environment, search out the egalitarian clues by looking at *The College Handbook* to find the percentage of students in fraternities and the percentage of ethnic groups. Look in *The Fiske Guide to Colleges* to learn how much emphasis is placed on varsity athletics compared to the sports participation of students on non-varsity teams. All of these things together build an image of the campus culture.

Once you have a list of colleges, you may question what to do next. How should you present yourself for admission? How up front should you be about being LGBTQ? What will hurt your chances for admission at the colleges you want to attend? Within the application process, a crucial question that you have to ask yourself is this: "Should I write about my sexual orientation in my college essay?"

> ▶ ▶ ▶ **WHEN LEADERSHIP FOR** *student government and major activities are controlled by independents as well as by fraternities, the chances increase for an egalitarian environment. Any campus that condones exclusivity in social life and student activities is not a safe place for the excluded.*

Many parents of gay high school students and college admissions officers advise gay students not to write about being GLBTQ.

Even though writing often helps students feel better, it will usually be to your advantage not to write your college essay about being gay—just as other minorities don't get in by definition, even if they are a recruited underrepresented group. The key word here is "usually." If you have been a gay activist leader in your school and state and have started, for example, a gay-straight alliance club, then it's easy to see that writing about this experience will make sense. If you have been a leader in your high school's GLBT activist club, have demonstrated the courage it takes to take on such a public role, and have stood up for what is not a teenage value, then you have truly distinguished yourself as a leader. Leadership is your strength. But if the essay is the more typical "poor me," "it's not fair" expression of a victim mentality, then most often it just won't stand up in the college essay competition. In those few moments when you have the focused attention of the college admissions dean, you must highlight your uniqueness and achievements as they will play out in the college community rather than focusing on your experience or feelings of discrimination or victimization.

Finally, research campus cultures carefully. Look for a history of egalitarian principles. Look for low fraternity numbers. Beware of what you are getting into. Check out the LGBT resources on the particular college campuses that you are considering. Your own perceptions of your sexuality and sexuality issues can change drastically in your first years away from home.

If you have any other special interests, check in your guidance office, in major bookstores, and online for guides that focus on a particular topic. You can find guides for conservative colleges, athletes' colleges, historically black colleges, women's colleges, and more.

Online Searches, View Books, and College Catalogs

The first thing that you receive from a college when you make an inquiry, visit their campus, sign a card at a fair, or score a certain number on the PSATs (whose lists are sold to colleges), is their view book.

View Books

Please keep in mind when you read college guides, watch videos, and go online to college websites that you are seeing the marketing arm of the college and university. It's the hard sell with Madison Avenue marketing glitz. Don't even think of choosing your college because some college sent you a brochure and personal letter inviting you to apply. Go ahead and read them. If you can distinguish one college from another through their view books, you're good! Just remember this: Always question who your sources are and what's in it for them. Some online homepages are not produced through admissions, and often the student newspaper is on the college website. So explore those homepages to see what students say and what they are doing and thinking about on campus.

College Catalog

The catalogs are another matter. Very few high school students take advantage of what they can learn about a college from the online course catalog. EVERY college to which you will apply has one! Take a look! College catalogs provide you with the list of courses and faculty at each college without pictures. Colleges seldom mention them. Students seldom look at them. As a counselor, one of my favorite exercises is to have a room of seniors with their laptops who have chosen their final list, and not yet written their applications. Students find the college catalog for the first application that they are going to write to answer the question, "Why do you want to come to Indiana U? Or Montana State U? Or Colgate?" The other time that seniors look at the catalog is when they are waitlisted, and again, it's to their advantage to know the college in depth and to be able to explain to the dean why it's such a great match.

When I meet with my students to talk about researching colleges, I take three colleges to explore their catalogs. Let's do it. You're sitting there in a seminar room; we're all around a conference table. A couple of you are seated on the window sills. They have all located the college catalogs on their screens: Goucher, Grinnell, and Guilford. Chances are that you may not have heard of any of these colleges, and if so, then good! That's the point—to get you to see many of America's outstanding colleges that you've never heard of. Let's say you are interested in theater arts. You know about the musical theater program at Syracuse and the acting program that takes only twenty students a year at Carnegie Mellon, and you have a friend at the Tisch School of New York University who says, "Oh, you have to come here!" OK. First we look at Goucher and we learn that it offers a theater major with six concentrations: general theater, performance, design and production, dramaturgy, directing and stage management, and arts adminis-tration. Next we learn that there are two professors doing all of that. Read through the course list and you will learn that there are twen-ty-four different courses offered in the department. Let's take a look at Grinnell's theater program, which is in the humanities division. There are six professors, although two are away on leave according to the cat-alog. Theater is an interdisciplinary major offering twenty-two cours-es including dance. Third, our last "G" catalog is Guilford's, where its theater studies program has three professors. Reading through this catalog you will learn that there are thirty course offerings, including dance and the history of theater. Do you see what's in the catalogs?

Get online after you have your final list of colleges, sit there for ten or fifteen minutes looking at the catalogs on your list and flip through one particular department just to get the idea of what kind of a re-source the catalogs are. When you are called upon to write an essay that details reasons you want to attend a particular college, remem-ber the college catalog. There is no better resource for writing why you want to go to that school, and you don't even need to know what your major is going to be to profit from the catalogs. Take the school subjects that you like best and look at the course offerings in French, environmental studies, and global development studies. What's that? Global development studies? Oh yeah, I see, at Grinnell they combine anthropology (we've heard of that before!), Chinese, English, French, history of South Africa, political science, religion, Spanish, and eco-nomics. WOW, I'd like that. Go ahead and tap the most underused, remarkably helpful resource in your college research—the college catalogs.

Online

You'll find everything online from registering for college tests to searching databases for a college list to scholarships to online applica-tions. If you don't have the website of the college you want to research, just Google it! When you look online, you'll come up with all kinds of information to get your search started and finished.

High school students also like the Princeton Review site (www.re-view.com). Enter your preference, courses, grades, and SATs. Then the college search will come up with a list of schools for you and offer information about each college that you have on your list. Check out

U.S. News & World Report (www.usnews.com) for the latest rankings and message boards. The biggest and most up-to-date is the College Board (www.collegeboard.com), which has all the general information you want to know, online applications, and college searches. Students love the Common App's YouTube videos! Students can now apply to more than 700 U.S. colleges and learn a lot of "how to's" for writing college applications from the YouTube videos found on their website: http://www.commonapp.org.

College Representatives Who Visit Your High School

Each year college representatives will visit many of your high schools. They come to talk about their colleges and to speak with you personally. Go to those meetings. It's an easy way to research the colleges. If you are a senior and you have a class when the college rep is scheduled to be at your school, ask your teacher if you may be excused in order to see the representative—especially if the college is one you are seriously considering. If you've already visited the college or had an interview at the college, you can say hello to the representative and relate your enthusiasm for attending the college. If you have an AP chemistry exam during the time the college dean is there, just zip by the college office to shake hands, say your name, and tell him that the AP chemistry is where you have to be. College reps love students who give priority to academics! A good impression, a face and name the representative will remember, and an informal meeting on your own territory go a long way toward influencing the college admissions dean.

Your High School Faculty

College alumni are a valuable resource for learning more about a specific college. Ask your teachers to tell you about the colleges they attended. Some of your teachers will have graduated recently; but even though you may think that some of your teachers are too old to remember their college days, keep in mind that campus cultures don't change that much. Even though issues may be different, the paraprofessionals vs. liberal arts, conservative vs. liberal campus cultures remain remarkably the same over the years.

College Visits

Spring break and summer vacation are good college visit times. Take the responsibility for arranging a family trip or a travel with a friend to see different types of colleges. You don't need to see all of the colleges on your list, as seeing some close to home will give you an idea for searching further. Senior year, however, is too late for all your college visits. Colleges usually have students on campus the last week of August and the first week of September, a perfect time to see colleges with students there if your school hasn't yet started. In the next chapter, we'll focus our attention on how to make the most of your visit to a college campus.

CHAPTER 4

THE COLLEGE VISIT

Visiting the colleges is the best way to research a school if you learn how to look and see. Seeing where you want to be a year from now and getting there is what this college selection process is all about. Remember the power is all in your hands when it comes to deciding where you are going to apply. The colleges will do everything in their power to get you to apply. Learning about the colleges will determine to which few of America's 2,400+ colleges you are going to send your strong, fascinating, unique, personalized application that will win the heart of the college admissions deans.

The campus visit will probably have a major impact on your college choice. For that reason, it's a very important part of your college research. If your family is driving near any college campus, it's never too early to look. An unofficial tour of the campus, joining a tour group, sitting in on an information session, or just hanging out in the student union can be worthwhile to you before official visits start in the spring of your junior year. Try for a variety of types of college cultures—big state, small liberal arts, conservative, liberal, Catholic, women's colleges—that is, if you're a young woman!

Scheduling the College Visit

Many a mother has called to ask me if she should schedule an interview when the family plans to visit colleges. My response is always, "I know how busy Jason is, I know that Julie is up to her ears in work, but the deans like to see the student, not their mother, take the initiative on college communications."

So, juniors, you can plan your trips with your parents, but you email the college rep to set up your college visit and an interview.

How to See

Once you've got a college visit scheduled, let's be clear about what you are doing there. Use your time on campus to look for data that you can't learn from the guides, virtual tours, alumni, or college fairs. When I take a busload of my juniors to two or three very different college environments every April, I remind them that they are there as anthropologists, which means we are there to see what is.

To see "what is" takes an open mind, a trained mind, a mind that collects data without judging, a mind that collects data in order to find some solutions or results or conclusions only after all the research is completed. An anthropologist is the opposite of a person that has drawn the conclusions before he collects the data and goes to visit a college to affirm those prejudgments. Do you remember what anthropologists do? They study how human societies function. They observe how one age group relates to another (students to faculty) and what the food is like. They detail the daily lives of people, separating out work (classes), play (sports and fraternities), community government (student government), priorities of the group culture (humanities, sciences, religious, entrepreneurial, athletic, artistic, fun and games, service to others), the architecture (look of the campus), and clothing (What do the T-shirts say? What do students wear to class? Do they dress differently to hang out? To go out?). Anthropologists always study the family structure, courtship, marriage obligations, and sexual behavior (Do students date? Do they hang out in groups? Are women safe on campus? What is the date-rape conversation on campus? Do gay students have a place in the mainstream on campus? Are there many married undergraduates?).

As you observe campus life for your eventual judgment of the college, look for some common threads that tie things together for you.

What did you like or not like about the campus culture? Were there students you talked to that you would like to get to know better? Were there students who gave you new insights? Did they seem like your kind of people? Does this campus strike you as a likely place for you next year? How did it feel to walk into a classroom building? What were kids like to each other in the student union? What was the conversation about in the dining room?

One of my students was sold on Haverford when he scanned the bulletin boards outside the dining hall and saw a $20 bill posted with a note that said "FOUND—in stacks on third floor library!" Honor code on a daily basis was important to this young man. Seeing it in action, in addition to hearing about it in the information session, was very convincing indeed. Haverford was clinched for Michael when he met with students in a group session. He commented, "I've never heard such truth about a place, and ease for being excited about pure academics, as I heard from that student session at Haverford last spring." Haverford's admissions director is the first one to tell students to look for the intangibles—the friendliness of everyone on campus, the excitement about academics—everything is grist for the mill. Michael is a good example of an anthropologist-in-training who collected his data from all the colleges on his long list, applied to eight colleges, was accepted by half of them, and had a hard time deciding between two. He went back to visit the two in late April of his senior year, before he had to make his May 1 decision. But it was the data he collected from that college visit in his junior year, his first time on any campus, on which he based his final decision.

Trust Your Gut

It's often hard for seniors to trust their gut when they are visiting college campuses. They have heard so many one-liners about the schools that they aren't sure if they are seeing something different than they heard. I remember our best soccer player in years at Nightingale. Laura loved team sports and wanted to go to one of America's great liberal arts colleges. After her visit to her favorite college, and learning that the only sports conversation Laura could get going was for boys' sports, she changed her mind and went to a different liberal arts college that wasn't even on her long list. Laura warned every junior in her class to be sure and visit the colleges before sending a deposit.

When you think of how decisions are made, your unconscious impressions should figure in. Your parents will understand that you can't always understand "why" you feel as you do. It's the same as when someone first walks into an apartment or house when looking at real estate and knows "this is the one." Sometimes one house or apartment will take right over—no explanation. In the case of a college visit, the same thing can happen. You might just "know" that you belong there.

Collecting the Data

Can you remember everything that you learn about your list of colleges? Of course you can't. It would be impossible to remember anything unless you create a system to organize your evaluation of the colleges. You will want to have some sort of simple form that won't be too much trouble to fill out. (Well, some of you are more detail oriented and will want a complex evaluation, so go for it!) But for the rest of us, a simple evaluation form for notes will be adequate. You can always add descriptions as you learn more about the college. Include your own short list of things that are important to you so you can be consistent in your evaluation of each campus you visit. You can start to use it as you read *Fiske* and *The Ultimate Guide to America's Best Colleges*.

Check out the College Data Evaluation Form that my students use. Some prefer it exactly as it is; others use it to create their own forms that match their curiosity and personality for collecting data.

COLLEGE DATA EVALUATION FORM

Name of College: _____

1. **What's most important to look for on this campus?**

   a) _____

   b) _____

   c) _____

   d) _____

2. **What's it like?**

   According to Fiske?
   _____
   _____
   _____
   _____

   According to *The Ultimate Guide to America's Best Colleges*?
   _____
   _____
   _____
   _____

   According to me?
   _____
   _____
   _____
   _____

   What's it like according to graduates from my high school?
   _____
   _____
   _____
   _____

   Other students on campus?
   _____
   _____
   _____
   _____

EVALUATION FORM

3. Can I get in?

Curriculum requirements according to the admissions dean:

_____
_____
_____
_____

Curriculum requirements according to my guidance counselor:

_____
_____
_____
_____

ACT/SAT score range according to the admissions dean and guide books:

_____
_____

ACT/SAT score range according to my guidance counselor:

_____
_____

4. What I like most about it:

_____
_____

5. What I don't like about it:

_____
_____

6. What my parents think about it:

_____
_____

7. Campus visit impression:

_____
_____

8. Interview impression:

_____
_____

Interviewer's name and email address:

_____
_____

EVALUATION FORM

9. **Can I pay for it?**

   Price per year: _____

   Financial aid forms required: _____

   Percentage of students receiving financial aid: _____

   Average amount of indebtedness for graduates: _____

   Director of Financial Aid:

   Phone: _____

   Email: _____

10. **If I apply:**

    Enter college on your College Application Organizer chart in Chapter 9.

Anthropologist in Training:
Observing the Natural Habitat of the College Student

If you lived in an ideal world and could collect all the data you wished for a perfect decision, you would stay overnight on each campus. That way, you could discover for yourself what the daily life is like and how weekend nights compare to weeknights. You would take a late-afternoon guided tour, have dinner, and stay overnight with a sophomore. You would go to some social, athletic, or cultural event that evening. Then you would get all your anthropologist antennae out to see what happens when everyone gets back to the dorm: Do they go to bed, sit around and talk, hit the email, argue, get on the phone? Next morning you would attend classes and hang out on campus. You would talk to the faculty, see the coaches, eat lunch and talk with students, have your scheduled interview, take some notes, and leave mid-afternoon for your next visit at a college nearby.

Again, that's ideal. No senior with a life can see many colleges in that manner. Do try, however, to visit a variety of types of colleges with the time that you do have, and try to see no more than two colleges a day. Be sure to take notes while you are there, or you will never remember what you saw where. If you have a short time, your minimum goal should be to take a student tour, attend an information session, and have an interview. These things should be arranged ahead of time.

Plan some time for the student union and talk to students who are not paid by the admissions dean. You might even look around the library to see who is there. In my many years of visiting hundreds of college campuses, I always head first for the library, to the reference section where daily newspapers are kept. Many colleges have easy chairs, couches, and wonderful places to sit down, put your feet up, and check your emails. The newspaper section varies from only *The New York Times* and *Wall Street Journal* to foreign newspapers such as *The Financial Times* from London, the *China Daily* from Beijing, *Le Figaro* and *Le Monde* from Paris, *Republico* from Rome, and the financial news from Sydney and Tokyo.

While you are in the library, take notice of the rule on open or closed stacks (students respect the books enough to be allowed to be among them without restrictions) and check the hours—they will range from open twenty-four hours a day and seven days a week to being closed on Saturday night and Sunday morning. Don't judge. Collect your data, and when you're going over your notes a few months later, your library and student union visit may make a difference in deciding whether you want to apply there.

If you were on an ideal college tour, you would eat at least two breakfasts, lunches, and dinners in the dining hall. That would give you a real impression of the food, a feeling for who sits where, and a sense of what dining hall behavior is like. When I went to visit one of my freshmen at Franklin and Marshall, she met me from across a large dining hall with a shout, "Hi, Ms. Mitchell, do you want to see where all the black kids sit?"

Alicia, who moved to New York City from Puerto Rico when she was in third grade, is the kind of young woman who loves to talk race. And, in fact, that is her distinguishing characteristic and why Franklin and Marshall was so eager to get her there: That's one kind of minority student that colleges search for, the one who gets the race conversations going whether students and faculty are ready for them or not. "Sure, Alicia, show me where all the black kids sit," I answered. "And did you know that that is the name of a book?"

So, juniors and seniors, look around those dining halls and notice if the athletes and fraternity brothers are all sitting in one place, if most students are eating alone, or if they are sitting in twos, or if they are at long tables with a gender and ethnic mix. What's it like? Remember you are looking for what you want to find there, not some combination that others tell you is best. It's your comfort level that you are after here. Just because you are a woman doesn't mean you want to be in a women's college or sitting with all the women in the dining room. If you are Hispanic, you may not necessarily want to find a place with great diversity; the strength of the chemistry department may be more important to you.

I remember a black student from Newark Academy who was accepted at Princeton and Amherst, and while he wanted to go to Princeton, he was fearful of all the racist things he had heard about the campus life. Finally, he decided that the English department's strength was worth more to him than the lack of diversity on campus. Just because everyone is talking about something, that doesn't mean the issue is the most important thing to you.

Take a Campus Tour—and Ask Lots of Questions

Plan ahead and arrange a campus tour as a part of your college visit. Look up some of your high school alumni who are there. If you let them know in plenty of time, they will often take you to class with them. See your guidance counselor to find out who's there from your high school.

When you arrive at the college to take your tour, remember to ask the student guide as many questions as you can think of. Students are the best sources of information that you can find to answer questions about a college culture.

Here are some questions that may get you started on your own student data collection:

> ➢ How large are your classes?

> ➢ Who teaches you? Can you get help from the professors?

> ➢ Who teaches the lab sections?

> ➢ Where do you study? Do you ever study in the library?

> ➢ Who grades your exams?

- ➢ Do kids talk a lot about grades?

- ➢ Have you ever been in a faculty home? How often?

- ➢ Do you talk much about national politics and issues?

- ➢ Do you belong to a fraternity/sorority? Are most of your friends in Greek life?

- ➢ Where can I get a copy of the campus newspaper?

- ➢ What do you like best/worst about being a student here?

- ➢ Where do most of the students hang out?

- ➢ What would you change about this college?

- ➢ What's the biggest student issue around here?

Do not make the mistake of trying to visit too many colleges on one trip. Do, however, visit a variety of different types of colleges; this should help you clarify your thoughts in the decision-making process.

Before you get carried away with too much time away from school for your college visits, keep in mind that the most important thing you can do to get into college is to get the very best academic record that you can. With your own academic record in mind, get out to as many college campuses as time and money will allow, but don't let your grades suffer.

CHAPTER 5

COMMUNICATIONS: PERSONALIZE, PERSONALIZE, PERSONALIZE

Now here you are, ready for step number three in the college selection process: communicating what you know about yourself to the deans of admissions in the colleges where you want to go. Think first that you will need a team to do the best job with these communications. Few students get into a highly selective college on their own. Finding advocates—those people who will go to bat for you from your high school and in the colleges where you apply—is an important strategy that must always be in your plan to win the dean's heart. Your teachers, parents, guidance counselor, coaches, drama and music teachers, and the college rep are all on this team.

Communicating the Academic Record and Balanced List to Parents

Every spring, juniors at the schools where I have worked bring their parents in for a college conference. This occurs after spring break and before the end of their junior year. By this time, each junior has written a one-page self-assessment, has researched at least twenty colleges, and has visited two colleges with the class to learn how to "see" a new culture. Most have also visited one or two more colleges with their parents, attended a college fair, looked online at the colleges' homepages, and talked to lots of seniors who know most about the colleges. Chances are, by the time the college conference rolls around, the students know a lot more about the colleges than their parents do.

In case you don't have a formal college program at your high school, let's run through this conference so that you get an idea of where you should be by spring of junior year. Here's what it looks like: We'll put Jake at the head of the table because he is the symbolic and true leader of the team helping him in his college search. We begin with going over everyone's responsibilities in the college selection process from spring of junior year until final list time in October of senior year. Jake's one and only responsibility, other than to do his very best academically, is to figure out what he really likes. The question he needs to ask himself with regard to each college is not "Can I get in?" but "Do I *want* to get in to this particular college?" His parents' responsibility is to help him keep an open mind, as everyone he knows will try to tell him where he should go to school. My responsibility as college advisor is to balance his list in the fall so that he ends up with eight applications to colleges he likes. These colleges will have a range of selectivity; that is, they will range from schools where he has a 25 percent chance of getting in to schools where he has a 90 percent chance of getting in.

Next, we go over his curriculum for his senior year, keeping in mind Jake's perception of himself as a student, which has emerged as he has articulated what he is looking for in a college and in the one-page introduction that he wrote for me. By his grades and teacher comments and conferences, we know his high school teachers' perception of Jake as a student. The unknown factor is the colleges' perception of Jake as a student. How will the colleges look at Jake? Going over his senior curriculum is the best way to evaluate his academic record from the college dean's perspective. Jake is taking English, calculus, AP French, AP Latin, and AP European history. The colleges will ask the college advisor, "Is this senior in the most rigorous curriculum offered in his high school?" They will look at each subject and—with Jake's high school profile in hand—see that AP English isn't offered, and all of the seniors take the same English, so yes, the English course that Jake is taking is the most rigorous offered. The college dean will also look for top mathematics, science, and foreign language. In Jake's case, the college admissions committee will note that he doesn't have the top-level mathematics course and there is no science in senior year. "A verbal guy," they say to themselves.

Back to our conference: Next, we look at the PSATs. I'll comment, "If your SAT math doesn't get up to a 650, why not give it another try in December of your senior year after you've been in calculus class for four months?" Then we go over Jake's long college list. He explains what he likes and doesn't like, and why. He tells us what he knows about each college and what his sources of information are. Jake and his parents are then advised to go forth into the world of college campuses and visit as many campus cultures as is feasible before the fall of Jake's senior year.

Communication Means Personalizing

Personalizing the college selection process in this age of number crunching is the strategy that will most likely help you win admission over other qualified applicants. This approach wins the heart of the college admissions dean. In order to win that heart, however, you must first have the numbers so that the dean is interested in learning more about the person behind those numbers. There are two personalizing strategies for getting in where you want to go, strategies that you cannot do without. Take a look at them:

> ➤ Make a friend of your guidance counselor.

> ➤ Make a friend of the college admissions dean (the regional representative who reads and evaluates your application and comes to your high school).

First, it is important to make a friend of your guidance counselor (college advisor) because she is the one who will be communicating (or not communicating) about you with the colleges on your list. No matter how inefficient, busy, or unfriendly your guidance counselor appears to be to you, you must make an effort to turn that around and make a friend of her. When the college has a question about your application, they will not call you, your coach, your outside consultant, or your favorite teacher—they will call your guidance counselor.

You need her advocacy. The college process is a one-time opportunity. This is no time for attitude. The college selection process is the place where you will grow up enough to leave home. Making a friend of someone you don't know or don't especially like is a great leap toward the maturity and character you will need as soon as you leave home.

> ▶▶▶ **PERSONALIZING THE COLLEGE** *selection process in this age of number crunching is the strategy that will most likely help you win admission over other qualified applicants.*

Second, make a friend of the college representative who is responsible for your high school. In the fall, the college reps fan out across America and the rest of the world to visit seniors in their own high schools or in some central place where they invite students from all the high schools around. They go to Europe, Eastern Europe, Australia, New Zealand, South America, and China seeking the brightest talent and best mix for their college's next freshman class. Even if you have an AP calculus class, make time for the college rep. If you want to go to Boston College, get yourself in to say hello to Howard Singer for five minutes, give him an academic reason why you love BC, and the academic reason why you can't stay to learn more. When you go on campus at Trinity College and Dean Angel Perez is in a meeting and can't see you, you leave a note and say, "I'm so and so, a senior from such and such, and I'm on your campus today. Sorry that I didn't get a chance to talk with you." When you live in Texas, and you know you aren't going to get a chance to visit Penn, call or write Dean Eric Furda and ask who the representative for your Texas high school is. When you find out that Seth Allen is both the Director of Admissions and the Pomona rep for your high school, you can become Seth Allen's email pal.

Making a friend of the college rep isn't just for the Ivies and small, selective colleges. College admissions people are interesting educators; they love young people, and they want to build the best possible class. Get to know them! Remember that they are going to choose a few from the thousands of qualified applicants who want to go to their college. The better they know who you are, the faster their hand will go up to vote for you around that admissions' committee table.

Even the huge public universities like Indiana, Maryland, Michigan, Virginia, and UNC: Chapel Hill have a representative responsible for out-of-state high schools. Director of Admissions at Indiana calls high school seniors at home to ask if she can answer any questions about her university. Vice President and former Director of Admissions Linda Clement at Maryland sent personal notes to high school applicants. Erica Sanders, Director of Admissions at Michigan, sends her admissions officers out to high schools with graduating classes of thirty as well as two thousand. Stephen Farmer of UNC: Chapel Hill writes personal notes to high school counselors. Dean Gregory Roberts at the University of Virginia gives personal tours to parents and seniors who come on campus to see his university. Don't know the names of the Deans and Directors of Admissions? Just Google the college and find out!

There is no excuse for not making a friend of the college rep at the eight colleges where you will apply. Every letter, every classroom-corrected essay, every question, every email, and every portfolio of photography or poems or short stories should be directed to this one person. Also arrange for your campus visit and interview through this admissions officer. You can't possibly win the heart of the college admissions dean without knowing his name or the name of your high school representative from each college on your list. Get those six or eight names from your counselor, or go online and look for the college admissions office and the name of the college rep who handles your high school. Every college admissions office is online.

Having said that personalizing is the only way to win the heart of the dean, we all know, (don't we?) that too much of a good thing never accomplishes the goal. With that in mind, consider that too much personalizing produces overkill, and overkill will do you in. Last year's graduating class made a lot of mistakes in their college applications according to the *news media*. Here are some of them: boring essays, long resumes with little commitment, and too many pointless emails and phone calls from students and their parents. Now we all know that you can't control your parents, but certainly you can be sure that your essays are personal, not travelogues or sports stories; that your resumes are not a laundry list of every club you ever attended, but that you use the space to say what you *learned* from your activities; and that you are never guilty of "admissions stalking!"

What's the Dean Looking For?

When you communicate—whether it is filling out your applications, writing your essay, or visiting the campus for an interview—you must consider what the college deans are looking for when admitting their freshman class. While they differ in whom they take, they all use a similar basic yardstick to evaluate their applicant pool.

General Evaluation

Each applicant is evaluated by several readers within the admissions office and given an overall rating. The rating number is then brought to a committee meeting, where a decision is made by all the admissions staff (these are the college representatives who come to your high schools, attend college fairs, and run the information sessions on their campuses). Before the admissions decision is made, the staff usually starts with evaluating six important parts to every applicant's file:

1. Transcript–rigor of curriculum and grades

2. Test scores

3. Application and essay

4. Teacher recommendations

5. High school recommendation

6. Other: interview, coach's ratings, special talent, outside recommendations

Let's be clear about the evaluation of your file. As Duke's Director of Admissions, Christoph Guttentag, pointed out to me, these six parts are not equal. There is nothing that counts as heavily as your transcript, that is, which courses you have taken and how well you have done. Colleges put your academic work at the top of their evaluation process.

Next are your test scores. Your SAT or ACT scores, usually supported by your SAT Subject Test scores, have been verified over time as a reliable predictor of college success when evaluated along with high school grades.

Your application and essay are also valuable tools in the evaluation process. They show how well you write and how clearly you think. A creative essay can easily distinguish you from your classmates.

Recommendations are very important, as teachers are the only people who have had direct contact with you as a student. They can write about your curiosity, motivation, dedication, effort, and all of those things that the dean is eager to evaluate. Because of that, you will want to choose teachers whom you think will write the strongest recommendations you can get. Your guidance counselor's responsibility is to write a letter representing your high school that will summarize your academic work, speak of your personality and character, incorporate your parent letter if you have one, and highlight your special talents.

Interviews, coach's ratings, activities, and special talent are usually important. But keep in mind that unless you are a national champion in writing, acting, line backing, or cello, your extracurricular talents will never substitute for meeting the college's academic requirements.

Knowing what colleges "usually" do in the admissions process gives you some background for asking questions about the specific colleges that interest you. For example, even though many selective colleges evaluate in six areas, the Rice University of Texas dean says that Rice is looking at five rating areas: the degree of difficulty of the curriculum, academic grades, school support (that means the guidance counselor's letter of recommendation), presentation (application, essay, interview), and personal qualities (character, maturity, judgment). At Rice, a regional college admissions officer first reads and evaluates the applicant. (The regional college admissions officer is the college rep who visits your high school, is at all of the college fairs in your city, and is your advocate in the admissions committee. This is the guy whose name and email address you know because you are going to make a friend of him no matter what, remember?)

The second reader in the Rice evaluation process is someone who reads not by region but on a national level. This allows the committee member the opportunity to get beyond personal experience with the high school and student. When one of my students visits a college campus and comes back disappointed that he didn't get to see the regional officer who is responsible for our high school (but instead met someone else in the admissions office), I am always happy because it adds one more person around the admissions decision-making table who has met this student. All the admissions staff has the same vote, whether they are regional director, dean, first year or thirty-fifth year committee member on the job! And of course my student left a note to his regional rep saying she was on campus and gave some academic observation that impressed her while she was there.

Academic Evaluation

What does looking at and evaluating the academics mean to these deans? To give you a clear understanding of what the Ivies and their selective friends are looking for in their application pool of students from all over the world, let's take a look at the rating scale at Princeton, because (along with Harvard, Columbia, and Stanford) they've got the "toughest of the tough" when it comes to admissions standards. If you know what Princeton considers the highest rating, a "one"—they rate on a scale from one to five—then you know the most rigorous scenario for getting in. When Princeton reps talk to juniors and their parents from the top New York City private (independent) schools, he says that he looks at the strength of the curriculum, the grades, and test scores. "A one," says the dean, "is somebody with five or six scores over 700 (SAT and SAT Subject Tests), mostly A's, a 4.0 average, and at least twenty solids. A 'solid' means an honors course, or an AP or IB course, or the most competitive level within the department." For example, some small high schools give only one English course, but if 100 percent of those students go on to competitive four-year colleges, that's considered a solid. On the other hand, if only 75 percent go on to a competitive four-year college, the course may not be considered a solid in Princeton's book.

Needless to say, there are not many academic "ones" in any college's applicant pool. To rate an academic "two", a senior must have twenty solids with a 3.9 average as well as five or six SATs over 700. Half of Columbia, Harvard, Princeton, Yale, and Stanford's applicant pool are usually twos or threes. It takes a "one" to distinguish oneself from the pack of twos and threes.

▶▶▶ **ADMISSIONS COMMITTEES ARE** *always looking for the strongest points in your folder—things that set you apart from other applicants, ways that you distinguish yourself from your classmates. Your special talents are what make you interesting. Colleges look for a well-rounded class, not a group of well-rounded students. Distinguish yourself!*

Standing Out: Special Talent

Special talent can make a big difference. We think of sports, because sports are often the most-talked-about talent, but each of you has some special talent that you will want to highlight on your own application. Some of you are outstanding musicians, writers, actors, poets, editors, innovators, photographers, and leaders. Others of you have a strong social conscience, unique hobbies, or an unusual background. Maybe being highly organized or committed to community service is your special talent. Admissions committees are always looking for the strongest points in your folder—things that set you apart from other applicants, ways that you distinguish yourself from your classmates. Your special talents are what make you interesting. Colleges look for a well-rounded class, not a group of well-rounded students. Distinguish yourself!

How does a student win the heart of the admissions dean once the numbers are in place? Or as Penn's Director of Graduate School of Education Eric J. Kaplan asks, "Amid all of those shifting currents, what do those of us who make decisions value most in a candidate? First of all, we want to see academic commitment and initiative, a rigorous scholastic record, and demonstrated excellence in non-classroom activities." Then the question becomes, how excellent is excellent in non-classroom activities? Let's turn to Princeton again to find out how they measure excellence in non-classroom activities. The rating systems for both academic and non-academic achievement are on a scale from one to five. Now listen to this, all you presidents of your class, presidents of your student council, quarterbacks of your football team that led your team to the state championship: to get a "one" in non-academics at Princeton (or Harvard, Yale, Columbia, and Stanford, the most selective colleges in the United States), you have to do something truly exceptional, such as making the junior Olympic team, founding a start-up business about to go public, holding a patent, publishing a book, or acting on Broadway. *That's* a "one." That's the national or international arena of competition.

It takes a state or regional achievement to rate a "two": Eastern states tennis rating, equestrian rating, football team winning the Western division, Central states regional band, Southwestern rodeo champion, Eagle Scout leader of Florida, top clarinetist in the North-Central states. *That's* a "two." Still pretty competitive, wouldn't you say?

Now a "three" is no slouch either! A three is tops in your own high school. If you are from a big, top academic suburban public high school, you know how much talent, time, and focus it takes to be captain of the Newton-North team, founder of Atlanta high school's LGBT club, editor of Seattle's high school yearbook, president of Cleveland's Ecumenical Youth Council, first violin in the Los Angeles high school's orchestra. That's a "three" in Ivy competition.

You will get a "four" in the Ivy pool if you are active (but don't show any particular leadership skills) in sports, belong to clubs, and play in the band. A "five" is usually given to students with very little non-academic achievement. Most applicants are "threes." Since you know the time, loyalty, and commitment leadership roles take, you might have assumed that leadership in your competitive high school would bring a much higher rating than it does. But you must consider your achievements as compared to students from other states and even foreign countries. Think on a world-wide scale as you assess the competition for admission. After all, that's what the evaluation is—an international measure as opposed to a measure by your own teachers and school. Don't get overwhelmed by the thought. Your responsibility is to do your best with your own interests, abilities, and values. Finding authentic seventeen-year-old students with their own voices is very high on the list of top picks for deans of admissions.

> ▶▶▶ **FINDING AUTHENTIC SEVENTEEN-YEAR-OLD**
> *students with their own voices is very high on the list*
> *of top picks for deans of admissions.*

CHAPTER 6

COLLEGE ECONOMICS 101

How much will it really cost?

You have to worry how financial aid talk influences your possibility for admission, and you should know that most students get some kind of financial aid. The deans have a pot of gold from which they must bring in a freshman class that meets all of the institutional priorities. The problem is, with the rising cost of a college education, families have never had to think about spending current college expenses as they must today. You should know, though, that each institution sets its own priorities for the makeup of its freshman class. These priorities include scholars, athletes, leadership positions, minorities, legacies, and international students. Do not believe the "hearsay" that money is not available for middle- and upper-income families. It all depends on whom the college wants in its class as well as on the number of children in your family, home mortgages, health needs of your family, and many other complex and variable factors. Check it out for yourself. Now is the time to start learning about hard ball in big-time finance. We are talking a major investment here—that could be more than your family ever thought of for your college education.

Paying for college used to be mostly an issue for your parents. Nowadays, students are more likely to take out school loans than parents. That means you are usually the one who ends up with years of debt. Many government loans are for students—not parents—so even though your parents may take on many of the costs of college for you, there are some things you must do yourself. Being well informed about college finances is one more way that you can show the dean of admissions that you are grown up and responsible enough to go to his selective college.

The average tuition and fees at an in-state public college is about 73 percent less than the average sticker price at a private college, at $10,116 for the year compared with $36,801, respectively, according to *U.S. News*. Among ranked private colleges, 120 charge sticker prices of at least $50,000 for the academic year, according to tuition and fees data reported to *U.S. News* by 785 private institutions. Only a few ranked private colleges and universities–61–list a full rate price of less than $20,000 in 2020.

Six College Money Principles

Here are six college money principles to help you understand your financial responsibility:

1. You won't have any idea how much a college will cost until you receive your financial aid package. Convince your parents that this is true. Do not select your final list by the advertised cost of the college.

2. You have to get your forms in early, and at best, on time to be competitive for the money.

3. Understand the meaning of "gapping." Even though college personnel know you can't afford to attend their college, they will still admit you; but they will not offer you the financial package that you need to go there. In other words, there will often be a "gap" between what you need and what they offer.

4. Negotiation with a better financial package from another college in hand is the way to go.

5. Don't be afraid of reasonable indebtedness. Reasonable is the key word here.

6. There is a "best" financial aid website. Here it is: www.finaid. org. It PAYS to check it out.

Now, let's take each of the six college money principles from the top and explore them one by one:

1. Research the cost.

Many parents hit the roof when their daughter says, "I want to go to Amherst or Smith College, and it costs $86,605 a year." Don't take "There is no way we are paying $86,605 a year for your education when you can go to UMass:Amherst as an in-state student for $32,868!" for an answer! Check it out. If Smith or Amherst is a perfect match for you, apply and fill out your financial aid forms. Then wait and see your Student Aid Reports (SARs) and how much your parents are expected to pay (Expected Family Contribution—EFC) before you start arguing.

Save the fights until you can say, "Look, Mom and Pop, here are the numbers. Not what you thought, huh?" Then make your case for your college. To get started on what the colleges think your parents can afford, go ahead and calculate the EFC online. The College Board (www.collegeboard.org) has the easiest format to use. Throughout the college selection process, always try to remember how the college perceives your application. A rough estimate of what your family is expected to pay gets you started on what the dean of admissions thinks it will cost the college to get you. For example, a college may expect you to bring in $9,000 a year on your own. This includes a $3,000 government loan, $3,000 from a campus work-study job and summer work, and savings for the third $3,000. Therefore the college usually includes a student work-study program in your financial package, which guarantees that you can earn a certain amount for the year.

2. Get your financial aid forms in on time.

The first step in the financial aid process, even before you apply, is to check with the colleges and ask which financial aid forms they require. Free Application for Federal Student Aid (FAFSA), the federal form that everyone needs to submit, is available in November from your guidance office or online at www.fafsa.ed.gov. A helpful brochure, The Student Guide: Financial Aid from the U.S. Department of Education can be requested from the same address. All lenders of federal and state money—federal Title IV student aid, Pell Grants, Stafford Loans, Supplemental Educational Opportunity Grants, College Work-Study, and the Perkins Loans—require that you complete the FAFSA. The FAFSA must be filed as close to January 1 as possible. Plan to use your parents' last year's income tax forms to estimate next year's income in order to get it in early. Don't even think of waiting until current taxes are ready before sending in your FAFSA form. No doubt about it—you won't get anywhere without the FAFSA properly filled out and sent in as close to January 1 as possible. (Don't send it before January 1, or it will be sent back and you will go to the end of the money line at most colleges.)

As many as eight hundred private, selective colleges and scholarship programs require the PROFILE form from the College Scholarship Service—the CSS. You must register for the PROFILE after you know your final list of colleges. You can get the registration form in your guidance office or online at www.collegeboard.org where you will find the online registration and application. Besides the PROFILE, remember that all federal and state money programs also require the FAFSA. Most of you will need work-study jobs, so both forms will often be required at the PROFILE colleges. Hard to believe but true, some colleges will also have their own forms in addition to the FAFSA and PROFILE. You will often need to complete the colleges' own financial aid forms to be competitive for the money. Before you give up on this deluge of forms and join the Foreign Legion instead of going to college, the good news is that they all want the same data. Once you have your parents at the kitchen table with their last year's income tax records, complete just the FAFSA form first. With the satisfaction of having completed the FAFSA, you will find that the other two forms are a piece of cake.

Again, don't even think of sending in any forms without first making several copies. Many a financial aid form gets held up or lost. In the meantime, the colleges will ask you for a copy of your FAFSA or PROFILE forms to use at the college financial aid office while they wait for the official form to arrive from the government or ETS. You will have an extra copy for them!

3. Understand "gapping," "financial aid," and "merit."

Most financial aid is awarded based on the financial need of the family. Given that the cost of college is going up every year and soaring, most colleges can no longer afford to accept or deny without knowing the paying ability of the student. Merit, or giving out their money according to whom they want in their college (institutional priorities) regardless of need, is the way colleges get higher test scores and special talents for their college. Using their "pot of gold" for merit means that the college money is going to bring in the students that they want most: high testers to get their ratings up, high grades to get their profiles up, underrepresented groups for diversity, as well as students with special talents to upgrade their orchestra or pitching team. A few selective colleges with high enough endowments and few enough families of need applying are able to meet 100 percent of the need of their students. The high cost of college is a national issue, and some politicians are trying to get relief in our state colleges and universities for American families.

▶ ▶ ▶ *THE BEST SOURCE for learning about your possibilities for receiving aid is with the director of financial aid. He can be as important to you as the dean of admissions. Make a friend of the director of financial aid early in the application process. Meet him. Know his name. Get his email address.*

The hard truth nowadays though is that most of that gold is given out for merit. It pays for you to be aware that when merit scholarships are up, meeting the financial need of many of the applicants is down.

The best source for learning about your possibilities for receiving aid is with the director of financial aid. He can be as important to you as the dean of admissions. Make a friend of the director of financial aid early in the application process. Meet him. Know his name. Get his email address.

4. Negotiate the package that is right for you.

Negotiating a workable financial aid package is important if you have one package that is out of line with the rest, and if you would give anything—except $50,000 indebtedness—to go to that college. Take the time to check out the possibility of getting a reevaluation of your financial need by the college. One of my students was offered financial help from one Ivy League school where she applied, all the while knowing that her first choice was Brown. She was disappointed to receive an offer of $10,000 less aid from Brown since that was the school she really wanted to attend most. The student made an appointment with the director of financial aid at Brown a few days before May 1. She took the better package from the other school with her for her Brown meeting. Then she explained that Brown was where she most wanted to be and asked them to reevaluate her case.

Not only did Brown match the other school's package, but they came up with a few thousand dollars more. Her family financial circumstances could be interpreted in a variety of ways, and because she was from an underrepresented group that Brown wanted on campus, she won the negotiation. Not everyone gets a match of their best package, and more often than not, the bigger package comes from where you do want to go. But if the package doesn't make sense to you, take the time to visit or call the director of financial aid and give negotiation a serious try. Hey, they won't take away what you already have because you asked for more!

5. Don't be afraid of reasonable indebtedness.

What's reasonable? Big-time college indebtedness is new since your parents' generation went to college. Nowadays the average undergraduate indebtedness at graduation is $46,600. Think about it. Have a figure in mind of how much is reasonable for you, partly depending on what career plans you have. Check out how much debt college graduates are incurring this year. If it's only $8,000, it doesn't sound like much—but that's $8,000 times four, which amounts to $32,000 in the end. On the other hand, we are talking about the equivalent of the price of a new car. Still, if you pay that debt off in the first five years of work (when you have your lowest salary), you will have to be paying a college debt each month on top of rent and on top of a car payment, and that's big money to a fledgling budget!

I had a student who "had" to go to Duke until she realized the size of her indebtedness at the end of four years. Thinking it over, Abigail realized that just getting in to Duke satisfied her "prestige need," and she decided to go one year to a City University of New York school. By living at home, she was able to attend college for $15,922 including tuition, mandatory fees, books, daily transportation, lunch, and personal expenses. Abigail was so surprised that she liked it so much that she stayed for four years! She completed her degree at Hunter College (CUNY) with honors. She and her family will end up with absolutely no debt. Abigail can now afford to go to graduate school or to work and get her master's degree on the side.

You must examine those financial packages. How much is grant or scholarship money (not to be paid back)? How much is student and family contribution? How much comes from loans (to be paid back)? Count up the indebtedness for four years. Think again about your final college decision in terms of four-year indebtedness.

Watch for colleges that load up on the debt; be aware of those colleges whose graduates leave with the least debt. There are a few colleges where students finish with debt figures that are lower than most, an average debt under $18,000. These schools are Amherst, Beloit, Grinnell, and Rice. Indebtedness is a worthy question in April when you are deciding where to go. Be sure to ask the college rep in the fall, "What's the average debt of this year's graduates?"

6. Go online for your financial aid research.

The very best Web site to help you in your financial considerations is found at www.finaid.org. There is hardly a question that can't be answered through it. Use this Web site to uncover and discover every single path that will lead to your share of the pot of gold!

Last Word on Financial Aid

After your family, the colleges are your major financial resource. But don't stop there. Another significant monetary source for your college tuition may be your parents' employer, church, or service club.

Get in touch with the director of financial aid as soon as you send in your application. Learn the director's name, make a friend, find out how the financial aid office can help you make your final decision on where you will go to college. Ask about the average financial package at each college, what percentage of students receive financial aid (the lower the percent, the better your chances are of getting more money), and the average graduate's indebtedness. *The Ultimate Guide to*

America's Best Colleges and *Paying for College Without Going Broke* cite the percentage of students receiving financial aid in bold letters—you can't miss it!

CHAPTER 7

FINAL LIST:
EIGHT FIRST CHOICES

You've assessed your curriculum, grades, test scores, and values. You've researched the colleges and know what they're like. You know how much your family is willing to pay for college. And now that November is here—it's final list time. November and December are the months when you must figure out to which colleges you are going to apply. First-term senior year is when you plan your strategies to win the heart of the college admissions deans in order to get the most number of choices for next April. Selecting which colleges are best for you after assessing your own ideas of what you want in a college and researching the colleges does not mean that you are sure which colleges you would like best. You could always spend more time researching, but at some point, you must stop collecting data and make some decisions—ready or not. The college application process has a time frame.

Between your junior and senior years, you will research about twenty colleges that sound best for you. You'll assess the kind of educational and campus environment where you will be happiest and most productive. You will then select a shorter list of colleges that are consistent with the type of school you want and that differ only in the selectivity for admissions. It makes sense to apply only to colleges where you have a reasonable chance for acceptance.

This is not the time that you actually choose where you will go to college. Don't get into fights at home at final list time about where you are—or are not—going to attend school. Wait until you hear from the colleges. Many seniors ruin their last year at home arguing about whether they will go to Rice or Cal Tech. Then in April, they learn that they didn't get in to either college, wasting all of that family life that could have been wonderful for everyone in the senior year.

Fall is the time that you set up your options in order to get choices in April—or a decision in December if you are applying early. Let's say you have at least ten or twelve colleges in mind for your final eight. You will soon realize, as all scientists do who collect data, that your research is never complete. Anthropologists know that there is always more to learn about a culture. You will keep learning more and more about yourself and your colleges until May 1 when you send in your deposit for a place in the freshman class. But by November or December of your senior year, you must narrow your college list to your final eight (or five or six or ten).

Do You Want to Get In?

As you look at your list of twenty colleges and begin to narrow your choices, the first question to ask yourself is not, "Can I get in?" but "Do I want to get in?" Consider what you have learned from your research. What have you found out regarding campus culture? Is this the environment where you will be happiest and most productive? The next question is, "Can I get in?" What are your chances of getting in with your numbers? Will the college be impressed with your grades from your high school?

How can you be sure you have two or three options next April? You can't go by the general guidelines of grades and SATs listed in the guidebooks. Those numbers are "in general," from "average" high schools. The college admissions deans know the different high schools. They will take only A's from some high schools, and dip to B's and C's at others because they know that the competition varies from school to school. The deans accept a great range of SAT and ACT scores. Remember that no test score will get you in. Remember too, that an

ACT 29 and SAT 1360 won't keep you out of anywhere. The counselor or teacher who helps students in your high school with the college process has to help you with the question of where you can get in. That means figuring out the chances of admission for eight colleges, knowing who gets in which colleges from the past two or three years with your numbers, and from your high school. You will want to balance your list in terms of selectivity for admission, not balance between big and small, East and West, urban and rural. Your final eight should be all the things you value most, and the main difference between them is only the selectivity for admission.

Balancing your final list requires experience and information. You want to keep your mind open in the process, so don't use emotionally loaded labels for the colleges on your list. You should know that no one gets to go to a "dream school" and nobody wants to go to a "safety school." For example, you probably haven't heard a senior in May proudly saying, "I'm going to my safety school." Let's agree to use numbers instead of labels to describe that final list.

Numbers, percentages, or odds are determined by the college decisions made for your particular high school in past years. Your guidance counselor can make an educated guess, using the statistics of your graduating class for the past two or three years. Your list should include one or two colleges where you have a 25 percent chance to get in; two or three with odds of 50 percent; one or two 75 percent's; and one or two where your counselor feels you have a 90 percent chance of getting in—all places you want to go. No one needs a college on his final list just because he can get in. If you can't think of eight places you want to go, go back to the guidebooks and research the colleges until you do. You've got over 2,400 four-year accredited colleges to choose from and three hundred of the top 10 percent colleges to search for in the *Ultimate* or Fiske guides!

When you figure out your numbers, you will often ask your guidance counselor, "Aren't I allowed just one dream school?" while actually thinking, "I'll beat the odds. I'll make Chicago, Pomona, and the University of Virginia. I'll be sorry all my life if I don't give it a try." At the same time, your counselor knows that the dream school is pure fantasy, out of the ballpark. We are not talking here about a 10 percent chance to get into a so-called "reach" college. We are not talking here about a legacy, a development case, a minority student, a full-pay international student, a major athlete, or the first violin from the Cincinnati orchestra either. We are talking here about the second quintile, solid B student in a very competitive, suburban high school, with two or three APs, a 675 critical reading and 685 math who has all-state sports, who was class president, and who performed top-of-the-line community service—and who doesn't have a prayer for Harvard, MIT, and Stanford. Not a prayer. Or the same student with calculus or AP foreign languages who won't hold up for the first cut at Cornell, Wesleyan, Northwestern, or the University of Texas. We may also be talking about the nicest kid in the world—the one who overcame the "overcomeable" obstacles of learning disabilities, a sister in a bulimic institute, a brother kicked out of prep school for drinking, the favorite of the whole faculty.

What is wrong with one or two dream schools on the final list? Here is what is wrong. A dream school is a definite deny to the counselor but not to the student. The student and his parents only appease the counselor and say that they will be sure to learn about other colleges. But in the end, they learn only more about Dream U. So, when college talk comes up at home, in the car, at the mall, at Thanksgiving dinner, at the cocktail party, "She is applying to Stanford" silences all future conversation about the other colleges. "We have to get in our Stanford application" is all that sinks in.

The real danger is that you will never get engaged in learning about the other colleges on your list. Duke's Director of Admissions Christoph Guttentag agrees. He tells me that he can't count the numbers of times that students and their parents say to him, "I applied to other schools, but I never thought I'd have to go to them. I only wanted to come to Duke."

"If only those students had researched the other colleges on their list, if only they had become excited about all of their college list, they wouldn't be as let down when two or three of the denials come rolling in," cautions Guttentag.

Let's say that Davidson is on your list and yet your curriculum and grades don't stand up to Davidson's competition for admission. Even though you have the facts in front of you, you keep learning more and more about Davidson. You spend your senior year thinking you just *have* to get into your dream school, even if you act cool about it to your counselor, who suggests you research some less competitive colleges.

Every college visit is back to Davidson. You compare all the other colleges on your list to the one that you will never be able to attend. You keep comparing those other top colleges on your final list—Rhodes, Rollins, and Richmond—to your view of Davidson. You judge rather than collect data. You jump to conclusions that are contrary to fact and without regard to the evidence. You will come up disappointed in April because in November you closed your mind to the terrific possibilities you had with your academic record and values. The goal of this final list is to yield two or three college choices where you really want to go. You are playing hard ball here, and you want each pitch to count. Don't throw away the few pitches in the strike zone because you don't like the sound of the name!

> ▶▶▶ **THE GOAL OF** *this final list is to yield two or three college choices where you really want to go.*

As you prepare your final list of eight colleges, it is hard to realize that colleges are more than their competitive level for admission. Because Middlebury is harder to get into than Connecticut College, Macalester, and Colorado College doesn't make Middlebury better! If you go to Colorado College, chances are very high that by Christmas time of your freshman year, you will wonder what ever possessed you to think that Middlebury was the one and only place for you. Because it's easier to get into the University of Oregon and Ohio State than it is to get into Berkeley and the University of Virginia doesn't mean that smart kids aren't challenged there. After all, a university is composed of many colleges, each with varying admission standards. The popularity of a university often inflates the competition for admission. This is the pure economics of supply and demand. It has nothing to do with being better—better means numbers in freshman classes, access to professors and to the courses you want, quality of campus housing, quality of life outside the classroom, numbers of students going on to graduate schools or graduating with jobs in outstanding training programs. Think of colleges as stock. Why invest in an overvalued college? Usually "overvalued" means you've heard a lot about it, and its name is on the tip of everyone's tongue. Why? Often because of its football and basketball teams—it seldom has anything to do with freshman courses.

Eight First Choices: The Final Eight

Let's be clear on the goal for your final list. You are not choosing, now, where you will go. You are after the greatest number of college options possible in April. Looking at your list as the options you want next April frees you to get to know a lot more about all of those colleges on your list. You will like best what you know best. If an older brother is at Johns Hopkins, that's best. If you went to soccer camp at Skidmore, that's best. If your favorite college team is Duke or Notre Dame, they're the best! Don't learn more and more about one or two colleges and think that you *have* to go to Beloit or Lake Forest. Get to know best all eight colleges on your final list.

> ►►► **YOU WILL LIKE** *best what you know best. Get to know best all eight colleges on your final list.*

In order to get to know best all of the colleges on your list, try very hard not to prioritize your final selections. If you think, "I have eight first choices," rather than a first, second, fifth, and eighth choice, you will put enthusiastic energy and thoughtful responses into all of your applications and essays. Many seniors have been shocked that they didn't get into what they considered the fourth, fifth, seventh, or eighth college on their list. Later they learned that the college found their application sloppy and that it showed that they had little interest in the college. This "don't prioritize" strategy will keep you writing meaningful applications with distinguishing short answers on all eight of the colleges on your final list, and you will respond with equal enthusiasm to six or eight college reps when they visit your high school this fall. Loving all eight colleges and letting the deans of admissions know of your high interest in each of them is the secret for creating the most number of April options in your senior year. You'll be smiling when you click on your computer and see a "We are pleased to inform you" come rolling in. You'll know you've won the hearts of several college admissions deans. If you manage to keep your mind open and to keep collecting the data after April—even after those acceptances come in—many of you will be surprised at what your final decision will be.

> ▶ ▶ ▶ **LOVING ALL EIGHT** *colleges and letting the deans of admissions know of your high interest in each of them is the secret for creating the most number of April options in your senior year.*

April 15: Now is the time to argue with your parents. You know the college decisions. You know what you want from a college, and you know your college cultures. April 15 until May 1 is when you build a strong case for where you want to go next year. The power is all yours.

One First Choice: Early Decision, Early Action, Restrictive Early Action

Flying in the face of "eight first choices" are the colleges' early plans. Harvard, Princeton, Stanford, Yale, and several other selective colleges have an early action single choice option. In recent years, colleges added all kinds of language to get students to apply early with VIP, personal, instant decisions, single choice "earlies," restricted choice "earlies," and all kinds of plans that promote an early decision for anxious students. This is college marketing. Don't get sucked in to believing that you have to go early!

Just for starters, don't even think about early decision until you have finalized your college list. Let's face it; early decision is great for the colleges. They lock in top testers who can pay the full cost early in the year. When they talk to you, you would almost think it was to your advantage to go early. But whoa! Let's look at the downside to an early plan. I know. I know. You are going to ask, "What have I got to lose?"

The college reps are out there hustling for as many applications as they can bring in. But there is another point of view for you to consider; it's from the applicant's side of the fence.

Besides the obvious things about early decision that hurt the student (a deferral or denial in December just before exams, being unable to learn more about the college match, basing your college admissions on your junior year and not waiting for senior grades and stronger

SATs)—everyone has to admit that it cuts decision time in half. The student has to know by October where he is applying. Then he must have the application in by November 1 or 15, depending on the school. The unqualified students for early decision (those who don't have the numbers to get in) have the impression that they will get in because of their high interest. "If we are really your first choice, then apply early!" is the clear message from most of the college admissions officers. This is said in information sessions to a general audience. There is no consideration for a student's individual standing. The rep doesn't have a clue about any particular student's academic record.

The worst part of early plans, however, is that early applications close minds. The student's primary task is to research the colleges to learn what's out there, to see the differences in campus cultures, to keep taking in data as an anthropologist or any scientist does in research. Students learn in science class that they must keep collecting data and evaluate only after all the data is in. This is no place for early judgment or guessing about a hypothesis ("I don't like this, I love that") before the data is in.

Let me tell you what happens to the research component in early decision: A senior will write to me in the summer and say, "I love Vassar, I'm going to apply early, I had an interview and it went on for an hour and twenty minutes." This student doesn't have the numbers to get into Vassar. I write back and say, "Doug, I know you love Vassar. Now let's go on and see what else you love. What is it that you like about Vassar? Here is a list of colleges just like it, with varying degrees of selectivity to get you started." All of that goes in one ear and out the other because the student (and this is very typical) only has eyes for Vassar. So he keeps learning more and more about that college. And remember? We all like best what we know best. When the student is denied or deferred in late December, not only can he not think straight because he is so surprised (regardless of how cool he may handle it), he just can't begin to open his mind at that late date. Some go through the motions, but they rarely get engaged in learning more about other colleges.

▶▶▶ **EARLY DECISIONS CLOSE** *minds. And a closed mind is the worst way to make a decision. It drastically* *shuts out the best possibilities for higher education. Learning how to make sound decisions is a major by-product of the college selection process.*

Your responsibility is to figure out what you really like, to come up with eight first choices. No one gets to know best their sixth, seventh, and eighth choice if they prioritize before they know their options—that is, before they know which colleges have admitted them and which have not. Students who have late decisions to make (those who have been placed on waitlists), often change their minds as to where they want to go because they have had the time to collect the data for several colleges. That's because they have been learning about the colleges with an open mind, and their parents have almost always given them permission to do so (that is, the parents didn't get stuck on their child's early choice).

So there you have it. Early decisions close minds. A closed mind is the worst way to make a decision. It drastically shuts out the best possibilities for higher education. Learning how to make sound decisions is a major by-product of the college selection process.

The early decision strategy usually helps the colleges a lot more than it helps students because early plans reduce your decision-making time by half. Getting the process "over with" doesn't begin to outweigh the advantages that learning more about the colleges and yourself during your senior year gives you. If you have a 10 to 25 percent chance of getting in to a certain school, and it's a competitive college on the national scene, don't buy in to the colleges' message to "Apply early if you clearly like it best." What harm will it do? Getting a deferral or a denial at exam time in December—with no acceptances from any other colleges to balance the denial—hurts. And it hurts a lot more in December than you think it will in September.

Here's another fact that is just as important: A very small percentage of those deferred students ever get in from the regular pool (5 to 10 percent). Think about it. Plain human behavior. If you read through an applicant's folder that you had turned down the first time, wouldn't you say to yourself, "Well, I didn't take her in the first round, wouldn't I rather say yes to a fresh, new applicant than the one I denied earlier?" Of course you would! We all would. Even though the colleges want to lock in the high flyers (top testers), and the media touts the national trend toward "earlies," it is never to your advantage unless you have what that college is looking for—the numbers. Of course I'll agree that there are always exceptions. It probably makes sense for about 10 percent of your class to apply early for one reason or another. If one of the colleges in your "50 percent chances to get in" stands out in high interest for you, or if financial aid or minority status is not a factor in your admissions, then it might make sense for you to consider applying early. The colleges talk to you only about your interest, but the flip side is that colleges act on your interest only if you have their numbers. If you aren't quite up there, don't even think of applying early. On the other hand, if you do have the numbers, you have researched your whole list, and you have considered the data you collected as an anthropologist would (rather than judging by hearsay and reputation), then early plans can give you a competitive edge over regular applicants because the college is assured that you will accept their offer.

PART II

Applying
to College

CHAPTER 8

COLLEGE ESSAY

When it comes time to write your college applications, you will see that the only thing that holds you back from completing them is your essay. Most of the application can be written in short spurts of time, between homework and school activities. The essay, however, takes a major amount of time, with many drafts to get it as well done as it needs to be. Once you have the numbers to get in, the essay and short answers are probably the most important part of your file.

Let's keep in mind that the Ivy deans are the first to say they turn away as many qualified and fascinating students as those they admit to their colleges. That's where your written work, the essay, comes in. If you've got the numbers that won't keep you out (please notice, all of you SAT buffs, numbers never get you in), there is one criterion above all others that tips the admissions committee toward a student. That single criterion is the ability to write—as demonstrated in your college essay, application, and short answers and in your classroom written papers. Some college admissions deans even ask to see the various drafts of senior classroom papers with teacher comments before they decide on the writing ability of the student. These admission staffs and committees take the time to look at what level of instruction you are getting in your high school, and they judge your writing ability by what you have learned from the opportunities you have been given.

Who Are You?

Your essay is a natural place to distinguish yourself from your classmates. Often it is read before the transcript is read, and the "you" of your essay is in the mind of the dean as he looks at your grades and the level of challenge you chose for your high school curriculum. Think carefully about the questions asked of you and spend the necessary time to formulate your response. This is your opportunity to communicate to the admissions committee who the person behind those numbers is—the real you. Just think, this is probably the only document for which the college admissions dean doesn't have a particular expectation. It is the only component of your college file that isn't already on your record. It is the part of your application where you can start from scratch today and make something special of yourself—just as you have in your academics for the past twelve years.

> ▶ ▶ ▶ **YOUR ESSAY IS** *a natural place to distinguish yourself from your classmates. This is your opportunity to communicate to the admissions committee who the person behind those numbers is—the real you. And this is probably the only document for which the college admissions dean doesn't have a particular expectation.*

Writing the Essay

Your college essay is your best opportunity to distinguish yourself from other applicants. You have a chance to show your ability to think and to write, and also to unveil your character, values, beliefs, and aspirations. It doesn't matter what your topic is, although the essay should not be a description of events. Here is what Harvard's Dean of Admissions William R. Fitzsimmons is looking for in a student essay: quality of thinking, questioning nature, openness to ideas, and unique expression of ideas. And if Bill Fitzsimmons is looking for those qualities in your essay, you can be sure you are on the right track with all the other college deans by adhering to Dean Fitzsimmons' standards.

Your college essay must be a lot more than a description of an event or activity; it must be an essay about what you've learned from an experience. No matter how technically correct your essay is, it's your creative intelligence that the college is trying to measure. After all, they have your English grades and test scores, so they know your ability to put words together. "It's the thoughts that you have, your unique way of putting ideas and events together, learning from literature, and your life of the mind that will distinguish you in the selective applicant pool," advises Harvard's Fitzsimmons.

Make the transition from assignments in English class to a personal writing style for your college essay. I have read hundreds of senior's first drafts, and all too often I must respond by saying, "Mr. English Teacher will love this. It's really well written, but it isn't right for a college admissions essay because it doesn't tell me who you are. It could be written by any teenager who said, 'everything will come out all right if only I try harder.' What about your struggle with geometry, your disappointment in your test scores, your breakup with your boyfriend, your love of French literature—now those are your things. Who are you, anyway, with all of those things going on? No one else in the applicant pool is going to have your take on those issues!"

Once the first draft is written, you know your perception of your essay. Now switch over and think how the college admissions dean will perceive your essay. You can't win the dean's heart if you don't know what he values! Always figure out your own perceptions of what you are doing in the process: on the application, at the interview, at the college fair, on your essay, and then switch your mind over to the perception and point of view of the college dean before you act.

What Deans of Admissions Look For

Let's hear it from the other side of the desk. An admissions officer wrote about current college essays in the *Chronicle of Higher Education*, the first and last daily word on college news. She says that *The Catcher in the Rye* is still the number one book that seniors write about, with *The Great Gatsby* coming in second. There are a lot of cultural identity books such as the Jewish kids writing about *The Chosen* or *Night*, and Indians writing about *Siddhartha*. Then there are all those white kids writing gee-whiz essays about *Invisible Man* and the Toni Morrison books. Jane Austin is a hit for an essay book for girls. "No surprises here," says the dean.

Most of the article, however, was about her astonishment and disappointment with the frequent citing of what she called "safe" books. You know them: motherhood and apple-pie books—all about love, friendship, long walks—nothing risky. This brings her article to the big question: "How come seventeen-year-olds never talk about relationships? Why can't they find a way to write about gender and sexuality?" She concludes her lament with "I guess these kids will continue to read safe books and we'll continue to read what they think about them." Now, seniors. Let that be a lesson to you. Don't write about the best sellers that all the other seniors will also cite in their essays! Just think how unique you'd be if you dared write about relationships and gender. While we're with the perceptions of the admissions officer, let's go right on and look at how a typical college admissions dean is looking at your essay.

Picture this: It's 6:55 p.m., dark and raining. A half-cup of cold coffee sits on the floor, leaning against a stack of essays. The dean has just finished reading seventy-eight college essays in one day, which she has tossed in another stack. She is late for her seven o'clock Friday night date. As she urges herself, "Read just one more before you go," she hastily grabs your essay.

If it's about environment, community service, or your favorite teacher, she groans before she even notices who wrote it. Think about it, how many essays do you think the deans will read about America's 2016 election of a president who had never held an elected office? If your essay's theme is one of the 3 Ds (divorce, depression, or drugs), she is in agony. If that "just one more before I go" essay is about Facebook, Twitter, or streaming favorites, watch out! If your essay is about God, love, injustice, death, or the purpose of life, it had better be funny! So...before you even get started on your college essay, give some serious thought to what's trendy, and then shy as far away as you can from it. No matter how unsure you are, try to trust your own personal story to write about.

A Reflection of You

Making the most of the essay is a reflection of how you are able to make the most of any opportunity that comes your way. It can also provide an expression of your attitudes and your understanding of the campus environment where you want to go.

> ▶ ▶ ▶ **BE YOURSELF AND** *go with the essay that has the most "you" in it, not necessarily the most academic or politically correct essay. Trust me. No—better yet, trust yourself!*

You have a chance to express the "you" that you know best and are most proud of. It doesn't matter what the question is or what topic you discuss. All the colleges want to know the same thing. What does this seventeen-year-old think? What has she learned about herself and the world, given the opportunities she has had in life? What kinds of learning attitudes and intellectual curiosity does he have? How confident is she? How "together," for a seventeen-year-old, is he? The answer to these questions can come from any topic.

More than a description of events, your college essay must tell how you feel about the event or activity, and what you've learned from the experience. In other words, if you write about your dad or grandmother, or a bike trip through China that you took last summer, or a community service job you held in Chile—no matter how dramatic—tell about the person or event in a short paragraph and use the rest of the essay to tell what you learned from the person or experience, or how you've changed because of it. Write about what you have learned about you, the world, and other people. No matter what the question—who or what has influenced you the most—the task is not to write about the "who" or the "what." The college admissions dean wants to know what fascinates you about the "who" or the "what." Your college essay documents how you stand out from your pals and all those other seniors applying to Selective U!

WRITING AND CONTENT TIPS FOR YOUR COLLEGE ESSAY

TIPS

- ➤ Write several drafts before the essay is final.

- ➤ Use all the standard rules of good writing. Be concise, be interesting, and use a "grabber" in the first line or paragraph to catch the attention of the readers. Remember: The readers will see thousands of high school senior essays. You want yours to stand out.

- ➤ Use a font big enough for the admissions staff to read easily. You do not want your essay to become tedious simply because the print is too small.

- ➤ Shorten the essay—not the spaces between the lines—to fit the essay into the required space. Most seniors have a hard time cutting down their essays; ask your English teacher to help you with that part.

- ➤ Many of you will want help with your essay. See your English teacher and your guidance counselor for both creative and technical help—that is, content ideas and correct grammar and spelling.

- ➤ Don't try to write what you think the committee wants to hear. Readers are not looking for something in particular; they are looking to learn more about who you are.

- ➤ The topic doesn't have to be dramatic or bizarre or unusual. You can write about the most ordinary daily activity you do or a story you read. It's what you learn and observe or how you've changed that counts.

- ➤ Never use the essay to tell why you have such poor grades, or how you know your next term will be better. An essay of excuses—no matter how valid—highlights your weaknesses. Your essay should always lead from your strengths. If you feel you have a good reason for poor grades, discuss it with your guidance counselor; she's the one to tell the colleges the reasons, not you.

The more selective the college, the more emphasis is usually placed on the essay. Good colleges expect good writers.

Most important, remember that English isn't just for English class! Apply the good writing skills you have learned in class. Make the transition from writing assignments in class to the writing of your essay. Tie in a literary reference, a character or event that you've read about. Integrating your personal statement with literature can be an interesting way to present your thoughts.

What's it going to be? The written word of a very interesting young person who is excited about going to college next year. If your teacher or counselor says it won't do (it's not up to your rigorous curriculum and grades), be quick to write another. Be prepared to rewrite a half dozen times. Technically correct won't make it; remember you may be the seventy-ninth applicant's essay read in that admissions dean's long, dreary day. You aren't boring. It's just that when teens get scared or anxious, they often write as if they are. You will want to send in a college essay that measures up to who you really are. Be yourself and go with the essay that has the most "you" in it, not necessarily the most academic or politically correct essay. Trust me. No—better yet, trust you!

CHAPTER 9

THE APPLICATION

The first written communication to the dean of college admissions will be your application. It is filed first—on top of everything else in your folder—and as far as the dean is concerned, that application is you. So be sure it looks as good as you get—spelling and grammar, neatness too! Writing your application is a major opportunity to distinguish yourself—to document your clarity, creativity, and competence. Everyone will tell you that the college essay is crucial to win the heart of the college admissions dean. That's true—but everyone knows it. What many are not aware of is that your college applications can be as creative as your essay.

College admissions deans read thousands of applications, so yours has to stand out—just like you do! I don't mean "stand out" in a quirky, gimmicky way, but in a "who you are" way. I teach my students an application strategy: Write not what the college can do for you; write what you can do for the college. The dean is looking for a strong freshman community that every high school senior in the world will want to be a part of. He wants a class that provides the college with high energy leadership in intellectual curiosity, publications, music, student government, athletics, creative thinking, and the arts.

Members of a college admissions staff read your application to evaluate if you are going to be a good match for the college and provide their community with any of those leadership categories they are seeking. If you have a high school record of integrating black and white students on the state or regional level, highlight it. The dean is checking to figure out how well you can handle freedom. If you are a political activist against drinking and drugs, say so! Colleges know they need as many aggressive nondrinkers as they can get. Let's take a closer look at the steps you must take in preparing your eight applications that hopefully will win the hearts of at least four college deans.

> ▶▶▶ **THE DEAN IS** *looking for a strong freshman community that every high school senior in the world will want to be a part of. He wants a class that provides the college with high energy leadership in intellectual curiosity, publications, music, student government, athletics, creative thinking, and the arts.*

Which Application Form Does the College Like Best?

Most colleges no longer have their own applications. There are several applications that students like because they can use the same online form for all of their colleges. You will hear about the Common App, the Universal App, the Coalition App, plus new application forms that may appear on the market. Students and their parents are always wondering which application does the college prefer? All you have to consider is this: the college is working to get as many freshman applications as possible. They don't care which one you use. As a school counselor, I always want my students to use the form on which they feel they can best describe themselves. That is, the form that gives them the most space to separate themselves from their classmates as a good fit for each particular college to which they are writing their application. When an application lists categories of activities, for example, and students have to use only lists of activities rather than what they learned from winning the chess championship in their state, they can look for a more flexible application where they can better describe their uniqueness. After all, the application is the best opportunity to separate themselves from all the other (academically) qualified applicants who are applying this year. Students need a flexible application to do that.

Which form is best? My students all know that I think that the application that a student likes best has a psychological edge. On the other hand, many school counselors have a huge student load for whom they must send in school records and recommendations. The last word on application forms: Check each college website on your list to see if they offer their own application or if they suggest a particular application form. And then check with your school (guidance or college) counselor. If the counselor has a preference, that is the one that you will use. No matter what form you use, remember this, all the other applicants have the same boxed-in application that you have to write. It's an even playing field.

Number of Applications

If your list is composed mostly of the top 10 percent of America's most selective colleges, you should plan to apply to no less than eight colleges with a range of competition for admission.

Read Chapter 7—Final List, and plan to choose two colleges in each category: schools where you have a 25 percent chance, 50 percent chance, 75 percent chance, and 90 percent chance to get in. Some students choose four 50 percents and no 25 percents. Others choose three 50s and three 75s, and two 90s. As long as you have at least two 75s and two 90s on your list, it doesn't matter how you distribute the 25s and 50s. When you are figuring out your competitive standing to get in, keep in mind that the colleges and demographics tell us that each year is going to be more competitive as more students apply.

Make sure that you are telling yourself the truth about your 90 percent chances on your final list. Try to evaluate your academic record as clearly as you can. It's hard to do, because so many seniors think that "senior grades are going to be better." They believe this wishful thinking will make it happen, or that hope and prayer will get them in. The dean of admissions doesn't see it that way; he goes by what your record is, not on what you hope for. Students with a B/C average and 25 ACT/620 SAT critical reading and math scores will not have a reasonable chance at the highly competitive colleges.

On the other side of the coin, don't apply to any college that you really don't want to attend. There is no sense in applying to University State College because it takes "everybody" and you want a place where you know you will get in if, in fact, you would never go there! I just can't begin to tell you how many seniors come to me in tears in April to say, "State College is the only place I got in, and I never wanted to go there." It's too late. You can't go back and research the colleges and get your application in by the January or February deadlines. So remember—you are working toward finding colleges that are consistent with your ideal college and have a range of selectivity for admissions. As Colgate's Dean of Admissions Gary Ross cautions, "Be sure you choose your 90s within your ideal campus cultures."

Writing the Application

When you look at the various applications and supplements that you have to complete, you're likely to think that it certainly doesn't look like the document that is going to win anyone's heart—and that's my point! Here's your chance to get an edge on those thousands of dull applications that all look alike and that the deans fall asleep reading: You are going to be creative with that boring application. You are going to "color outside the lines."

There are a lot of places on an application where you can distinguish yourself. One rule is that you must never leave anything blank. What if the question asks for academic honors and you don't have any? How about AP/IB courses? If nothing else, fill in that you have to meet academic requirements to take the AP/IB courses in your school (if you do, that is!). How about those Latin exams in ninth grade? If you really can't come up with anything, either draw a little line in the space, so the dean knows you saw the question, or better yet, write a phrase about how competitive your high school is, or some academic achievement that your school isn't formally calling an honor.

▶▶▶ **YOU ARE WORKING** *toward finding colleges that are consistent with your ideal college and have a range of selectivity for admissions.*

▶ ▶ ▶ **YOU ARE GOING** *to be creative with that boring application. You are going to "color outside the lines." There are a lot of places on an application where you can distinguish yourself.*

The activities section gives you a lot of latitude for distinguishing yourself. Don't bother with a lot of ninth grade activities that you have since dropped. Trinity's Admissions Dean Anthony Berry points out to applicants that the colleges are looking for long-term commitment to two or three activities. The purpose of many of the application's questions is to highlight how you spend your time outside the classroom. The dean wants to know about your leadership and involvement, and how much time you spend in that activity. Take the time to figure it out.

American college deans are always trying to measure character. Looking at how you spend your time and what you value gives deans and members of an admissions committee insight into who you are, the total person. Perhaps you have a passion for dance and choreography. Rather than fill in all the columns just as they appear on the application, use that space to do your own thing: Write a few sentences describing your time and leadership in dance.

When you are writing about your activities, think about what message you want to give those who read your entries. Add details that highlight your contributions. You're good? How good? You run? How fast? You play? What level of music do you play? You act? What plays were you in, and what were your roles? How much time did you spend in sports, on publications, in the performing arts? Give specifics. Which position do you play and how good is the team? How many goals did you score? You write? Where were you published? Has your school paper or yearbook won any national awards? Specificity is needed to show how you stand out from all the other qualified applicants. Details are key for your college rep to get a clear and complete picture of who you are. You won't win a heart without being specific.

Don't forget to include your paid jobs and unpaid home responsibilities. Harvard's Dean of Admissions Bill Fitzsimmons tells about a student from rural New England who didn't mention that he had to work on the family farm after school and every weekend because he thought, "A big shot college dean wouldn't want to know about ordinary labor." Wrong! Whether you are running the school newspaper, caring for younger siblings or a grandparent at home, food shopping for the family, or selling clothes at the Gap, the colleges want to know how you spend your time.

Use the application to write what you are crazy about but didn't write about in your essay. In other words, use the application questions as guidelines, not as rigid categories where you have to put exactly what they ask for.

Short Answers Call for Creativity

Besides the essay, the application often includes questions asking for short answers or single paragraph responses. Most students slide over these, but here's another opportunity for you to get the edge and to win a heart. The question, "Why are you applying to Wake Forest? Or Boston College? Or UC Santa Cruz?" is posed to get you to show them how well you know the college, how well you did your research. As an anthropologist who has been collecting data on this campus culture, you will do very well on this question! Sometimes the short-answer question is similar to one of these: "What do you expect your major will be?" or "What career have you chosen?" Never say or check undecided, and never write or check that you don't know.

"Wait. What if I am undecided and I don't know?" Well, of course, most of you are undecided or don't know, but you don't want to miss an opportunity to tell more about yourself. You are trying to give the dean of admissions real insight into who you are. Let's say you don't have a clue about your major. In that case, say something that you do know. For example, "I don't know where it will take me, but right now AP Latin is by far my favorite subject and the one I most enjoy studying." Or, "Everyone in my family says I should be a doctor because I love biology and chemistry, but all I know is that I want to keep learning more science; I don't know which science I'll like best in college." Or, "As much as I like the academics, I have to say that it's music that interests me most right now. I don't want to go to a music college or conservatory, but I do want to be sure there are plenty of music opportunities for me at college." See what I mean? Doesn't that make sense? The dean learns a lot more about you from what you do know about yourself than he would learn if you checked the undecided (lost opportunity) box.

▶ ▶ ▶ **NEVER SAY OR** *check undecided, and never write or check that you don't know.*

In summary, the application is an opportunity for you to shine and to establish who you are, what you value, how you spend your time, what kinds of academics you like best, and how well you can express yourself in a small space. Many students miss out on this chance to distinguish themselves from other applicants. If you put it right up there with the importance of the essay, you'll surely win the heart of the admissions dean who dreads reading most of the very ordinary applications that seniors manage to send in. Wake up those deans and admissions reps! They will love reading a creative application for a change. Get your own voice and personality into the application, as well as into your essay.

Supplementary Materials

The college application consists of the points that you fill in plus the materials that you ask others to send. Test scores, secondary school reports, mid term report, final report, and letters of recommendation are all supplementary materials that you are responsible for getting to the dean. Take a look at the best way to go about this responsibility.

Reporting Test Scores to Colleges

You are responsible for releasing your Score Choice scores and for having your official test scores sent from ETS or ACT to your colleges. If you have not listed your colleges on your SAT or ACT registration forms (the scores will be sent to four colleges that you designate at no extra charge), then you must telephone, go online, or pick up additional score report forms in the College Advising Office. Releasing Score Choice and reporting scores to the colleges are two different procedures. You are responsible for both. In order to fill out these score report forms, you must know your CEEB registration number (found on the blue student copy, which contains your scores and which you

College Application Organizer

College Name		Bates	Denison	Grinnell
College Representative		W. Mitchell	P. Robinson	J. Sumner
Email		admissions@ bates.edu	admissions@ denison.edu	askgrin@ grinnell.edu
Address		23 Campus Ave., Lewiston, ME 04240	Box H, Granville, OH 43023	PO Box 805, Grinnell, IA 50112
Part I (or Common Application Supplement)	Due Date	1/1	1/15	1/2
	Supplemental Essay (if any)	0	0	0
	Done	✓	✓	✓
	Xeroxed	✓	✓	✓
	Check/fee waiver	$60	$40	$30
	Sent	12/1	12/1	12/1
Teacher Recommendations	Ms. Schutt	11/12	11/12	11/12
	Mr. Fuller	11/12	11/12	11/12
Secondary School Report (SSR)		11/12	11/12	11/12
Midyear Report				
Part II	Due Date	2/1	2/1	1/20
	Essay #1	1/1	1/1	1/3
	Essay #2 (if any)	1/15	1/15	1/3
	Done	✓	✓	✓
	Checked (by you AND someone else)	Mr. Loughery	Mr. Loughery	Ms. Schutt
	Xeroxed	✓	✓	✓
	Postcard	✓	✓	✓
	Check/fee waiver (if there was no Part I)	✓	✓	✓
	Sent	1/25	1/25	12-Jan
Interview	Date	10/8	Alum 2/8	Alum 1/28
	Interviewer	W. Mitchell	M. Hills	NYC: J. Pei
	Thank you note	✓	✓	✓
College Testing Requirements (SAT, SAT Subject Tests, ACT, TOEFL)"		ACT; SAT; SAT Subject Tests optional; TOEFL or IELTS required for international	ACT or SAT optional; TOEFL or IELTS for international	ACT with Writing or SAT; TOEFL or IELTS for international
Extra Materials (DVDs, portfolios, additional recommendations)"		2/14	2/14	2/14
Application completed & sent		12/29	1/25	12/22

Haverford	Macalester	Middlebury	Pitzer	Wesleyan
M. Keaton	L. Robinson	R. Clagett	Perez	C. Thornton
admitme@ haverford.edu	admissions@ macalester.edu	admissions@ middlebury.edu	admissions@ pitzer.edu	admission@ wesleyan.edu
370 Lancaster Ave., Haverford, PA 19041	1600 Grand Ave., St. Paul, MN 55105	131 So. Main, Middlebury, VT 05753	1050 N. Mills Ave., Claremont, CA 91711	70 Wyllis Ave., Middletown, CT 06459
1/15	1/15	12/15	1/1	1/1
✓	0	✓	0	0
✓	✓	✓	✓	✓
✓	✓	✓	✓	✓
$60	$40	$65	$50	$55
12/10	12/10	12/1	12/10	12/10
11/20	11/20	11/12	11/20	11/20
11/20	11/20	11/12	11/20	11/20
11/20	11/20	11/12	11/20	11/20
1/15	1/13	12/15	2/1	1/1
1/3	1/3	12/1	1/1	12/1
1/3	1/3	12/1	1/15	12/1
✓	✓	✓	✓	✓
Mrs. Wheater	Mrs. Wheater	Ms. Schutt	Mr. Loughery	Ms. Schutt
✓	✓	✓	✓	✓
✓	✓	✓	✓	✓
✓	✓	✓	✓	✓
✓	✓	✓	✓	✓
10/20	11/15 school	10/9	2/6 alum	10/18
campus student	L. Robinson	C. Perine on campus	J. Larskin	Information session
✓	✓	✓	✓	✓
ACT with Writing or SAT; 2 SAT Subject Tests	ACT with Writing or SAT; SAT Subject Test optional; TOEFL or IELTS for international	SAT or ACT optional; TOEFL or IELTS for international	ACT or SAT optional; 2 SAT Subject Tests incl. Math recommended	ACT with Writing or SAT; 2 SAT Subject Tests
2/14	2/14	2/14	2/14	2/14
1/8	1/8	12/7	12/20	12/23

received in the mail) and the code numbers of the colleges to which you are applying (found online and in the SAT registration bulletin).

Before you make any decisions regarding what to do about senior year SAT Subject Tests, consider the perception of an Ivy dean of admissions. The college dean cautions students not to use Score Choice senior year. He writes, "This past year, by the time those applicants who had opted for Score Choice received their scores and only then asked the testing agency to release them to the colleges, many of the scores simply arrived too late, i.e., after the applications of many of those students had already been reviewed." Now listen. You don't want that to happen to you. Take the dean's advice and realize that many of the colleges use Superscores, that is, the two highest SAT Subject Test scores anyway, and therefore you aren't taking any risk, as they know your earlier scores. Not to mention that many students forget that they had opted for Score Choice when they registered, and never do send them in.

Secondary School Report Form

Most applications will have a Secondary School Report (SSR), Midterm, and Final Report form. Fill out the top part of these forms with your name, address, and senior year courses and get them to your school guidance office. Your Secondary School Report, Midterm and Final grades forms will be mailed to the college by your high school in time to meet your deadline and will include the following:

1. Transcript (including courses and grades).

2. Test data (unofficial only). Many high schools do not send a copy of your SAT or ACT scores because only those from ETS or ACT are official.

3. Your high school letter of recommendation signed by your principal or guidance counselor (college advisor), or both.

4. Your high school profile (a description of your school, information on test scores for your class, GPAs, grade distribution of your class, and a list of colleges where previous classes have matriculated).

5. Some high schools send teacher recommendations along with the other reports. Don't drive the school office crazy asking if

your SSR went out or not. On the other hand, it's reasonable for you to ask when you return from your winter holiday if your reports were mailed. You'll be happy to know that the dean of admissions does not hold you responsible for late transcripts and records that are sent from your school.

Teacher Recommendations

Most colleges require a teacher recommendation, and some require two. It is most important that you choose teachers who know you best to write your recommendations. Sometimes a college will specify that the recommendations come from particular teachers. Try to choose two teachers in different subject areas. Here's what you do:

1. Ask the teacher if she or he will write a recommendation for you.

2. Give the teacher the proper form filled in as requested. If your school counselor sends them with your school records, write the date needed and the name of the guidance or college counselor on the envelope. If the teacher is requested to send in her own recommendations, give her your form with an addressed, stamped envelope for each college. Be sure to allow the teacher plenty of time to write the recommendation. On the envelope, pencil in the deadline date for the particular college. A teacher usually writes one letter, photocopies it, and attaches the letter to each of the forms for different colleges. The same teachers will write all of your recommendations. Don't hesitate to ask them, as they will expect you to use them for all of your applications. Keep in mind that teachers have many recommendations to write. If you don't ask them early (allow three weeks for them to have the time to write it), many will have to say "no," simply because they are overcommitted with other college recommendations.

3. After you get your college decisions, share your acceptances with the teachers and thank them for writing their recommendations. They are pleased to write the letters for you but want to be kept up to date with the results.

Other Letters of Recommendation

It's tempting to send letters of recommendation from all of those people in high places who love you—your clergy, the cardinal of Nebraska, summer and after-school boss, U.S. senator, neighbors, your parent's senior law partner, the head doctor in the university lab who supervised your summer science project—but do not send more letters than requested unless the letter writers have a strong connection with that particular college. In most cases, reading those "love letters" just takes valuable time—time that could be better spent reading what you wrote on your application and in your essay and what your classroom teachers and school personnel shared about you.

On the other hand, having people in high places with a strong connection to the particular college write letters of recommendation can be a strategy that will make a big difference for qualified students. A college trustee is a strong connection. A friend of the university president is a strong connection. An alumnus or alumna who gives a lot of money to the college (development) is a strong connection. A grandparent is considered a legacy, and that is also a strong connection. If you have a sister currently at Northwestern, send her into the admissions office in mid-February to talk to your high school rep about you as a possible match for the campus. If your father graduated from Brown, or your mother from Holy Cross, their letters can make a difference. These letters should be short—one page. Letters are better than phone calls or emails because they will be added to your folder for more than one person on the committee to read. A phone call is easily lost in the thousands of pieces of paper flying around the admissions dean's office in February. And your legacy parents should write about you and what they know of the campus culture—in other words, how those two entities match. That's the part that they know best and that the college can't get from anybody else. All the strong connection letters should be sent around Valentine's Day (a little "winning the heart" symbolism can't hurt), close enough to decision time that the admissions committee won't forget and not too close to decision time when the deans are so crazed with overwork that they won't remember to file the letter.

Application Deadlines: Early, Rolling, and Regular

It used to be that most students applied to college at the same time—regular decision time. Now the majority of students get in on early or late decision plans; that is, they get in early or they come in late from the waitlist (after May 1). Many public universities get students in all year long, on what is called the "rolling" admissions plan. Let's take a closer look at what's best for you—not necessarily what everyone else is doing—but the best strategy for you to get the options you want.

Early Action (EA) and Restricted Early Action (REA)

First, there's early action (EA), a program whereby you will apply by the first or middle of November and will receive an early decision in mid-December. You are not obligated to enroll if admitted (you may also be denied or deferred early). Harvard, Yale, Princeton, Stanford, and Boston College used to be best known for EA; but the plot thickens! These highly selective colleges switched to "Restrictive or Single-Choice Early Action," meaning that you may apply only to their REA program, and not to any other early programs. Since then, others have joined in. To be clear, it means that you may apply only to one early program of any kind, but it differs from Early Decision in that you may apply to other colleges in their regular pool and you do not have to make your decision until May 1, as in the regular decision. Colleges who are still with the regular Early Action (EA) program include: Cal Tech, Chicago, Georgetown, MIT, UNC: Chapel Hill, and Notre Dame. Colleges change their categories for applications often. It is your responsibility to check each of your application deadlines. Do not go by a college guide or online website except those of the particular college where you will apply. The risk with Early Action programs is that you can be denied on the basis of your junior year and not deferred into their regular pool to be evaluated by your senior year record.

Early Decision (ED)

The early plan that you hear most about is early decision (ED). In this program you apply by the first or middle of November and receive an early decision in mid-December. You are obligated to enroll if admitted (if the financial aid is sufficient) and to withdraw all other college applications. You may also be denied or deferred. Increasingly, colleges are offering a second or "late" early decision, applying in

January with decisions given in February, and some even a "late-late" early decision.

In the past few years and growing, there are more early plans with different names than anyone can possibly keep track of. You will find "Priority," "VIP," "Snap Apps," "Instant Decision," "Candidate's Choice" plans, special plans, and you-name-it plans! Why so many programs and plans? Colleges want to get those applications in and start reading them as early in the fall as they can get them. And early plans are wonderful for colleges, but they can be awful for students who aren't ready to make those decisions. The colleges are looking to get the top testers and full-paying students locked in, which is what EA does for them. Early plans at selective colleges are for outstanding students. There's a myth out there that it's "easier" to get in early. The Ivies have much more competition in the early plan as do all of the other highly selective colleges. It just depends on which colleges you are talking about.

Highly selective colleges take 35 to 50 percent of their freshman class from students who utilize early decision plans. These students are the top dogs, crème de la crème, those with top grades in rigorous programs, and big-time testers. But Early plans are not for everyone. Let's suppose that you are not at the top and don't have the numbers for an early decision. Then you really don't have a chance in the tough early competition. And you are not allowed second thoughts about other colleges. Some applicants are rejected altogether; the result is that they are denied rather than deferred by mid-December, losing the opportunity to submit better test scores and higher grades earned during the senior year. It's also devastating to be rejected in December.

You don't have to apply early to let the college officials know their school is your first choice. If it's not to your advantage to apply early, find other ways to let the admissions committee know you believe you are a strong match with their school. Write it on your application or in your essay. Tell the admissions officer during your interview.

Talk over the early decision possibility carefully at home and with your school counselor. Check to verify that you have the "numbers" needed from your high school to get in early. ED is getting to be such a big thing that you also need to consider the downside. This is discussed in Chapter 7.

Rolling Admissions

Rolling admissions is an admissions policy by which the dean evaluates and decides upon applicants as soon as their application files are complete. This continues until the class is full. Colleges with rolling admissions usually promise a decision within six weeks. Public universities are often rolling, although they may hold the decision until spring for out-of-state students, and the dates tend to vary each year.

Some colleges consider a complete file at the end of junior year, and others wait for first-term senior grades. Because many of the state universities are on rolling admissions, and students tend to apply early, some colleges may fill their housing and main campus by January. Here's the rule for rolling admissions: the sooner the better. If you have already decided that they are on your final list, your application for universities such as Indiana, Michigan, Penn State, and Wisconsin should be completed by November 1. Treat rolling admissions as early decision deadlines.

Sending Applications

It is your responsibility to send or mail your applications as soon as they are completed. Your high school will send your transcript, but you are responsible for telling your guidance counselor the deadlines by which each college must receive your grades and reports. Regardless of when your high school gets their records out, your applications should be sent as soon as you have filled them out. Be sure to get your application in before the deadline, and remember to save a copy before you send them so that you have back-up copies at home. Exceptions: There are a handful of colleges that want your school to send your application. In that case, your guidance office will send your part of the application and your application check together with the school reports.

Resist January Add-Ons

It's January of senior year. Your applications are in the mail. You have personalized the college process as best you can. You are well on your way to winning many college deans' hearts. There's nothing more to do. Now the long wait for early April has begun. The dreams have begun too. Seniors are famous for their college decision dreams; they begin from the moment that they mail their applications.

Then it is January. Seniors all over the country rush into their college counselor and say, "I'd better add just one more college." Your parents call your guidance counselor to say, "I was at a New Year's party and talked to my niece who goes to Cornell," or "I was talking to my sister at my nephew's bar mitzvah in Dallas—she has a neighbor who goes to Reed," or "My sister from Philadelphia, whose children go to Haverford, called and they thought that Susie should have applied there too. It's not too late, right?" What harm can one more application do?

Resist the temptation to send just one more application. The urge to apply to another college is the first sign of anxiety in the waiting process. It's true. Taking action helps reduce anxiety. But adding a college each month is not the most constructive action you can take. You have a college list. You have researched your possibilities, talked endlessly with your parents, your friends, teachers, and counselor. Your college list represents a consistency in type of college environment—those colleges where you will be most productive. It also represents a range in the competition for admissions. In other words, it's a balanced list. Adding another college from out of nowhere—often a suggestion from someone who doesn't have a clue about the logic of your choices—does not work toward the good of getting your best options.

> ▶▶▶ **RESIST THE TEMPTATION** *to send just one more application.*

There is, however, an important action you can take to quench that anxious feeling that you need to be doing something. That action is to concentrate on the colleges to which you have already applied. That action is designed to increase your odds for getting into the colleges on your list. You can begin right now by working harder on each subject you are taking.

College admissions deans will welcome significant new information about applicants before they make their decisions in mid-March. You can send an exceptional paper or report a significant achievement to the college dean before mid-March. You can write an unusual paper, compose a poem, a song, a short story; research an event in history; create a piece of art or painting; construct an outstanding experiment in science; win races on the swim team, establish a new basketball record; write a play in French, or tell about your independent study project. In other words, you can further distinguish yourself from the pack in some academic, athletic, leadership, or artistic way. Begin now—as soon as you have the urge to add another college to your college list. Talk with your teachers and ask them to help you to present a significant piece of new work to the college. Please note: The key word here is "significant." Significant doesn't mean more of the same. It doesn't mean to add quantity to what you have already sent the college rep or dean. Send something different from what you have already given them.

Let me tell you a sad story. Ben Z. applied to Columbia. He was right up there with his numbers: high 700s across the board, A and B+ record in a rigorous curriculum from a top competitive private school. He had sent a wonderful portfolio of his writing to the Columbia rep. The Columbia rep and I talked on the phone; Ben was looking good in the pool. Colleges love writers—male writers even have an edge, just as female mathematicians do. Ben couldn't control his waiting anxiety, so he brought me a stack of literary magazines and newspapers in which he had been published to send to the rep so the rep could really see how good he was. No amount of "The rep will hate that, Ben, admissions officers don't want a stack of magazines and newspapers, and besides that, you have already sent a terrific portfolio with most of those stories," could dissuade Ben from sending his magazines. A few days later the phone rings. "Joyce, I just received fifty pounds of scrap paper from your Ben. That's going to hurt him. Haven't you taught your students not to send me this kind of baled garbage that I have to get rid of?" Needless to say, Ben was denied at Columbia.

Don't waste your resources (time and energy) by falling prey to anxiety. When you start adding a college helter-skelter to your list, it appears to the college admissions staff that you are "running scared." Instead, build on the firm foundation you've been working on since first grade to establish your academic credibility. You have done a solid piece of work constructing your EIGHT FIRST CHOICES through self-assessment and college research. Be confident! Have courage! Send the college dean a significant piece of new work and then go out and run around your school track until you are ready to think about something else.

CHAPTER 10

THE INTERVIEW

S tudents tend to dread the college interview more than they do the dentist. When they come back to report about the interview, they are often disappointed because it turned out to be an information session selling the college rather than an interview for getting to know the student. Or other times students fly long distances to visit colleges and find that their interviews are with other students. Now that's the high school side of the issue. Macalester's Dean Lorne Robinson pointed out to me that their seniors are well-trained student interviewers and are very helpful to the process. Occidental's Vince Cuseo, Dean of Admissions, agreed that if students are interviewing applicants, it's very important for the high school student to know if it's an evaluative or an information-giving interview. Is it required or recommended?

▶ ▶ ▶ **YOUR PARENTS TEND** *to overrate the value of the interview, and the colleges tend to underrate them.*

The truth is that your parents tend to overrate the value of the interview, and the colleges tend to underrate them. You will notice that your parents will ask you a million interview questions, "Are you ready for the interview? Shouldn't you have a practice interview at a college where you won't apply? Does your guidance counselor give you practice interviews at school? Here—read this book on interviews!"

Parents just can't believe that their charming, fascinating, brilliant child will not wow the admissions dean and be accepted on the spot—if only she could have an interview with the dean of admissions. College deans, on the other hand, tend to say that the interview affirms the rest of the applicant's file, and unless they spot a freak, it doesn't usually make a difference in acceptance. But hey! Don't we all know by now that an unconscious power is always at work? And if the dean hits it off with you, won't he or she read your whole folder with a smile? Of course! Here is just one more opportunity to win the heart of the college admissions dean by personalizing your application. This is a chance to show the inner you behind your numbers.

But please, try not to read too much into the interview, such as "We were supposed to meet for thirty minutes and I was in there for over an hour!" A lot of disappointment comes out of hitting it off with the marketing man, who of course is friendly and interested, and putting forth his best efforts to get you to apply to his school—regardless of your academic record.

The Unconscious Power of the Interview

Let's face it, colleges are clear about what they are looking for in your application, essay, SAT scores, teacher recommendations, and the secondary school report. They are not so clear about what they want from your interview, if they want an interview, and who does the interview. And they are not at all clear about how they use the interview.

It's easy to agree that the use and value of an interview varies more than any other aspect of the college admissions process. Typical of the remarks made by the deans of admissions who give interviews is this one from Anne Springer, Bowdoin College admissions officer: "Evaluative interview notes are the last thing in the applicant's folder, and the admissions committee reads them last. If there is a discrepancy between the interview and the high school's recommendation, we call the guidance counselor; and if we can't reach anyone at the high school, we go with the school's report, knowing that we had a very short time with the student."

But, wait. Let's always remember this: What colleges say they want and what they want can be two separate things. In fact, what they wanted last year and what they want this year and will want next year are often three different things. Eric J. Kaplan at the University of Pennsylvania said, "I wish I could give unqualified answers, but I can't. And herein lies the frustration for all of the weary students and their parents. The objectives of an institution are like a moving target. They can change almost annually to reflect its priorities. One cannot adequately prepare to be a top candidate for an Ivy League college by cultivating a set of skills that meet today's priorities; tomorrow's may be very different."

Admissions deans, like most people, don't know how they make decisions. Add their different institutional priorities each year and they become moving targets. They often would not admit that their unconscious mind is fast at work, as their gut tells them what to do while their head spins quickly to catch up with a rationalization of "why" they decided what they did. This is true for how people buy a car, how they rent an apartment, choose a friend, and how admissions deans decide which 20 percent of the 80 percent qualified applicants will get into their freshman class.

Because of this human behavior trait, I make a point of teaching my high school seniors the unconscious part of the decision-making process once the numbers (curriculum, grades, and testing) are in place. I don't have to remind you that the selective colleges choose one-fourth and less of the qualified students who apply to their colleges. Even though the numbers of the freshman class will remain relatively the same, the numbers of college admissions officers reading applications aren't increasing to keep up with the rapidly increasing numbers of applicants. If you could sit around any selective college admissions' committee table, you would quickly learn that the hand of the admissions officer shoots up for a "YES!" if and when the student has personalized his or her application. It is the applicant that the dean recognizes that will get admitted from the qualified pool. Unlike what the SAT tutors want the public to think, it never comes down to making the choice based on a 735/32 verbal score winning over a 680/29. Once an applicant gets in the verbal 680/29 range, the numbers game is all over. That simply narrows the pool. When final choices are made from that pool, it's the student who wins the heart of the admissions dean who gets in.

The student who wins the dean's heart does it mostly through the application and the essay. After all, the written word documents how a student thinks. You can win the dean's heart through your application, although many students fall short—those short answers are too often written with great haste. In all too many instances, students miss the opportunity to win a heart by making a first impression on the application.

The Spoken Word

Coming right in there after the numbers and written word is the "spoken word" component. The spoken word comes in several forms: The interview is the most formal of the spoken word, but verbal interaction anywhere and any time can enhance the possibility of winning the heart of the admissions dean.

Interviews and getting together in person with a college admissions dean or rep at college fairs, college receptions, or college information sessions are opportunities for building relationships with college personnel. The college admissions dean's visit to your high school and your visit to the college campus are parts of the blah-blah factor (spoken word component). In other words, to win the dean's heart, you have to be aware of the verbal factor. Your verbal exchanges with the admissions dean go beyond the formal interview to include any time that the two of you have personal interaction whether it is on campus, at your high school, at the Yale Club in New York, at the Harvard Club in Chicago, or on neutral territory.

Who Requires What?

Nothing varies more from campus to campus than the interview policy. Consider, for example, that Colgate, Johns Hopkins, Stanford, Vanderbilt, and Vassar are all optional, and yet only Stanford and Vanderbilt are evaluative interviews, the others are informational. Most of the Ivies are required, but some are recommended. Some are informative only and yet others are evaluative. What does that tell you? You must check if the interview is required or recommended for each college. It is your responsibility to check online or ask the admissions rep for each of your colleges where you apply to answer these questions concerning their interviews:

> ➢ Is your college interview an information session—selling the college?

> ➢ Or is the student evaluated in the interview? And if so, is the interview evaluated on a numerical scale? Evaluated by an admissions officer, a student, or the alumnus?

> ➢ Would you categorize your school's interview as required, recommended, or non-existent?

> ➢ Is the admissions interview initiated by the student or the college?

The answers will be mixed. That makes interviews confusing for students and parents—confusing in that they vary a lot from college to college. And confusion produces anxiety. Let's see what you need to know about college interviews to cut through some of the confusion.

Some colleges say interviews count a lot. Some say they are information sessions and not real interviews. Some say they are just to keep the alumni happy. Some interviews are organized by students who have work-study jobs in the admissions office. Well, do they really count? It depends on the policy of the college: Is it a time to tell the student about the college, or is it an evaluative interview of the student's qualifications for admission? That may not be clear. So, the point for you to keep in mind is this. No matter what they say, the blah-blah factor always counts on some level.

How Do Interviews Count?

Well, what did you learn from this great variety of interview practices? How are you going to find out what the colleges where you have applied expect regarding interviews? Let me help you.

Here's what we know: The policies vary so much that you will have to ask the college admissions dean: (a) do you require or recommend an interview? (b) where and when can I get an interview? (c) is the interview evaluated? and (d) do I initiate the interview or does the college get in touch with me after I send in my application? Finally, if the colleges where you apply require or recommend an interview and if you live within three hours' drive of the college, request an interview on campus so that you can be counted as one applicant who is interested enough to come to campus for an interview.

It needn't be said that you won't be able to find a "right way" to interview. No matter which part of the process you are working on, you must always keep in mind that, given the great diversity of American colleges, these schools do not all want the same kind of student. Likewise, a particular college doesn't want their students all alike, and each year they may have different priorities for the students that they do want. As in the application and essay, your focus should be on finding and trusting your own voice; that is, the voice of a teenager telling the dean about his or her special interests and talents. Your written word (essay, application, classroom papers) and your spoken word (interview, college dean encounters) are found within you, not by copying the style of other students' essays or memorizing an interview format. What's in you is what the deans want to know.

> ▶▶▶ **DON'T DREAD THE** *interview.* *Think "conversation"—this is not a grilling session or a search for right answers.*

Juniors and seniors: Don't dread the interview. Think "conversation"—this is not a grilling session or a search for right answers. Whatever you say in the interview must make sense to you! If you aren't comfortable asking how this college differs from other ones that sound similar to you, don't ask that question. If you would rather talk about current events that you know well from reading a daily newspaper than discuss a book, turn the question around and talk about what you know best.

You will probably see more variation in the interview policy than in any other area of the application process. Just as you are responsible for knowing the particular tests required for each college, you are also responsible for knowing the interview policy for the schools on your list. When you're on campus, take a campus tour, attend an information session, see the dorms, find out where the students hang out, and talk to them. Ask to schedule an interview.

Colleges that require an interview will initiate the process after you have applied. Besides the on-campus interviews, others that you may well encounter are the student interview, the alumni interview, the group interview, the special-interest interview, the online interview, and the audition. (The special-interest and audition interviews are usually for the performing arts and sports.)

When you find out the policy of any particular college on your final list, you will learn which kind of an interview you will have. If you have a choice between an on-campus interview with the admissions staff or an off-campus alumni interview, always go with the on-campus or online interview with the admissions staff. Even though they both put an evaluative report into your folder, only the admissions staff sits around that committee table and raises their hands to say "yes" to your application. In all of these interviews, your goal is always the same: (a) to distinguish yourself and (b) to show a high level of interest in their college.

Have some hard facts at hand about the academics and any of your special interests in music, theater, sports, or publications, and have some hard questions to ask that aren't easily answered online or in the view books. Showing strong interest is more and more an important factor in being accepted by selective colleges.

Interview Tips

Read the college guides and course catalogs online ahead of time so that you will know important things about the college before you get to the interview. Have some questions in mind that are specific for that college. Be prepared to talk about your strengths and traits that need improvement, as well as your interests and special talents. Remember that interviews are a two-way exchange. Try to think of the interview as a conversation rather than a question-and-answer session.

TIPS

- ➤ Don't even think of taking your phone into an interview.

- ➤ Don't chew gum. Practice by not chewing gum when you go to college rep visits at your high school.

- ➤ Watch your language. Avoid the words "like" and "you know." At least cut down on the numbers of times you use these words.

➤ If you have a straight A record in AP courses, have taken twenty-three solids, have at least a 35 ACT and 1570 SAT scores, and have a book coming out on climate control, it doesn't matter too much what you wear. But if you're like most students with a little less than the above, a good impression always helps. Clean school clothes—nothing torn or ripped, no matter how fashionable that might be—are fine. Look "together." Arrive on time, shake hands firmly, sit and stand straight, and act confident and happy to be there. Cool doesn't sell. Sullen doesn't either; the dean will know that your mother made you be there.

➤ Admissions interviews are your opportunity to sell yourself. Make a friend of the interviewer. Look him in the eye. Be straightforward and relaxed in your conversation. Don't try to get at "what they want to hear." Be confident that there are no "right" answers or directions for the interview to go. The interviewers want to know you better. Mostly, they want to assess your attitude toward learning. But they also want to discover other qualities that will help you adapt to their campus. For example, do you have a sense of humor? Do you have the ability to overcome tough situations? Are you resilient after getting a bad grade, or do you get mad at the teacher and stop working? What do you know about this college? Are you the kind of student who can take advantage of the educational opportunities at this school? How high is your interest in attending this college? What kind of match will you make in this college community? How will you manage your time and life when you get away from home and on your own? How will you spend your out-of-class time? What are your values? Let your answers reflect the confidence you have in yourself. The more you like you, the more the interviewer (and others) will too!

➤ Have clear goals that you are able to discuss honestly. Some common questions they may ask are these: What interests

TIPS

you about this college? What are you looking for in a college? What are your educational goals? Why should we accept you? What do you expect to contribute to our college community?

➢ Don't give excuses for your grades or tell how you're going to do better next semester (wishful thinking). Lead from your strengths. For example, talk about your love for reading, for sports, for a beautiful campus, for Latin, or for politics. Share your pride in your family, your achievements, your dog-training techniques, your summer school experience, your snowboarding awards, your favorite newspaper, your favorite team, the business you started.

➢ Take time to listen to the questions and answer them directly. It's hard, but try not to worry about silence. Collect your thoughts. Tell the admissions personnel that you are eager to go to college and what you like about this college.

Go to the interview with your goal clearly in your mind: to set yourself apart from the other applicants and to be sure that the dean of admissions is clear that you are interested in getting into this college. Trust yourself. You are the one that the college wants to get to know, and if you are comfortable with the conversations that you have with the dean of admissions, you can be sure that you did well. Get right in there with the blah-blah factor every chance you have in order to distinguish that fascinating "you" behind your great numbers!

CHAPTER 11

LATE DECISION (WAITLISTED!)

High school seniors read and hear an awful lot of talk about early action, early decision, early notification, early priority, restricted early, early this and early that. I call it "first down." Sports talk. On the other hand, you never read or hear about late decision—or getting into college in June or July, having been accepted from the waitlist. I call *that* "stealing home." More sports talk. Getting in "off the waitlist" is the spring sport of the college application season.

Colleges don't like to talk about it. They don't include "late decision" in their information sessions with students and parents, but you should know about late decision because a significant percentage of the freshman class comes in from the waitlist. You should also know about late decisions before spring arrives with April letters informing you that you are on wait-list status. You have to be ready for late decision in order to take advantage of the process. Your mind must be open. Your psyche set. There's no giving up until the waitlist—the late decision—has closed.

A smaller and smaller proportion of incoming classes are getting into college on regular admission in April. Many selective colleges take up to and over 50 percent early. They also accept up to 33 percent of their class from the waitlist, so we are talking about a significant percentage of the class being admitted on either an early or late decision!

▶ ▶ ▶ **THE COLLEGE SELECTION** *process is a process that builds character. And character never builds quickly.*

When I tell a senior that he has a 50 percent chance to get into Johns Hopkins, for example, I mean before September, not necessarily as an early (December) or regular (April) acceptance. It is not to your advantage to "have to know" your college decision "early" in December or "regular" in April. You must be psyched ahead of time for the long haul, for the whole nine yards, and even for overtime if necessary. The college selection process is a process that, like any real challenge, builds character. And character never builds quickly.

Some years a lot more late decision (waitlist) activity happens than in other years. For example, the year that Harvard and Princeton no longer had an early plan, the most selective colleges in the country went for up to three hundred students on their May 1 waitlist. Whenever there is a new director of admissions or an interim director at a college, you can count on that sort of thing happening. If a college isn't sure of their "yield" (number of enrolled students from the accepted list), or if their yield is down and many chosen students do not accept their kind invitation for admittance, the colleges use the waitlist and late decision as a safety net.

A college can take as many as three hundred students from the waitlist to get the freshman numbers that they need. Because of a late decision, many a student goes to a college that's different from the one they had fantasized about all senior year. And yet when those waitlisted seniors learn more about that college option, they find that the waitlist worked better for them than their original preference. If you aren't sure that you want to attend the waitlisted college, you can decide what you want to do after you get off the waitlist. You will have a choice between the waitlisted and your "deposited" college, the college where you've already been accepted and paid the May 1 deposit that holds your spot in the incoming class. Many students ask—so let me answer the question formulating in your mind right here—if you get off the waitlist, you don't necessarily have to go to that college!

Let's say that you decide to stay on two waitlists. If you stay on a waitlist, you will want to do your best to be accepted. This means more than returning the requested card to accept wait-list status. Best effort means writing a letter along with the card that you return. In that short letter, tell the admissions dean that it's disappointing not to have been accepted. Give an academic reason why you are still interested in, for example, Wesleyan (and say something other than you love Connecticut or your best friend goes there). In the letter, add something new that the college doesn't know: provide latest grades (if they went up), enclose a graded English paper—even if it's not an A, it will document the kind of work you do and the kind of instruction you are receiving. Enclose a poem, short story, or school newspaper article that you wrote since you applied. And finally, end your letter with a statement that you want to be there in September.

Write that letter assuming you are going to get off the "wait" list and onto the "accept" list. In recent years, some waitlists were still moving in August, even though most colleges agree to close their wait-lists by June 30. If your wait-list college is the college you still want after all of your decisions are in, hang in there and keep sending something new to express your continued interest. Call or send something at least every two weeks, and keep your energy high when talking to the admissions dean. If you cared enough to apply in the first place, don't let up now and do half the job. Put your two best feet forward. Getting off the waitlist is like stealing home—it's a great challenge and fun!

▶ ▶ ▶ **GETTING OFF THE** *waitlist is like stealing home— it's a great challenge and fun!*

Sports talk is important. In fact, we can use an athlete's behavior and attitude as our model for getting accepted into college: Get in there and give your best. Be in good enough shape to stay until over-time has been played out. Be of the mind psychologically to go the extra inning after a tie—until a late decision has been made.

Early decision (first down) to regular decision (running the bases or picking up yardage) to late decision (stealing home) are the results of different strategies. Like athletes, you should go into the competition knowing the different strategies of the three separate ball games for the best advantage. Let's remember that America's top three hundred colleges have so many outstanding students applying that many of the "admit-list" and "wait-list" students are interchangeable. Colleges are looking for reasons to take one waitlisted student over another. It's up to you to give it to them!

CHAPTER 12

TRANSFERS

There are a lot of good reasons why students transfer. A student will tell you that she opted for a different course of study and another college had that major. Another student might say that he couldn't afford one college. But most often, although many students would never admit it, and some are not aware that they transfer because they didn't do the research and the college just wasn't a good match—they got there and didn't fit in. Don't worry about why you want to transfer. Transferring is big time in American colleges and universities.

I had a student from New York City that was dying to go to Colgate. She got there and found it "too rural," "too remote," and "too fraternity," so she transferred to Barnard (as a high school senior she swore she would never go to a woman's college). After a year at Barnard, she missed all her Colgate pals—the rural, the remote, the fraternities—so back she went to Colgate to earn her degree. Might I add that she is now a graduate student in religion at Columbia University (back to Barnard).

I had another student who was dying to go to Wesleyan, but he didn't get in. He went to a less competitive college where he took no math, no science, and no foreign language his first year. He got a B average and waltzed into Wesleyan his sophomore year. It's much easier to get into the selective colleges as a sophomore than as a freshman!

I spoke to a transfer student at a top public university who said he came for an architecture program, but they cut the program after his first semester there. I asked why he didn't transfer, and his response was, "Because I love it here."

A student transferred from Pitzer to Reed, where she became an art history major. At that time, however, there was no studio art major, which is what she decided she wanted. She stayed anyway because, as she put it, "It's where I want to be." (Studio art is currently the third largest major at Reed.)

Some students transfer because they change. One young man couldn't wait to go to Michigan for the Big Ten football games, the great variety of strong undergraduate courses, a big enough place where everyone *wouldn't* know his name and keep after him every minute. After two years of enjoying all of those things, he decided that he wanted a small, focused community where he could get in-depth conversation all the time about environmental issues, and so he transferred to Bowdoin.

▶▶▶ **A MAJOR IN** *English literature, mathematics, chemistry, biology, psychology, foreign language, economics, or religion leads to every career in the world.*

What's my point? When the match (campus culture to personality) is right, the program just doesn't make that much difference in a liberal arts college. A liberal arts degree closes no doors. Liberal arts leads to everything. A major in English literature, mathematics, chemistry, biology, psychology, foreign language, economics, or religion leads to every career in the world—even those careers yet to be hatched.

It doesn't matter why you want to transfer; what matters is that you have the freedom and the option to transfer and know how to go about it. Usually you can transfer up to two years of undergraduate work. Things are different in the application process for transfer students than they were in high school because you now have a college record. Usually the application is due in March or April for a fall transfer. Some colleges take a January transfer. Check it out with the admissions dean.

The new college will be more interested in your college grades than they will in your high school record or ACT/SATs (lucky you!). Even though the dean of admissions will be interested in what you did outside of the classroom, it's your personal statement that is read the most carefully after your college transcript. It has to be good. It has to be convincing. What did you learn about yourself and the world in those one or two years at college? Why do you want to transfer? Why do you especially want to transfer to the college to which you are applying? Be sure you have strong academic as well as personal reasons for the transfer—read the course catalog, meet a professor or two, and know what you are looking for.

Ask how many transfers are admitted. The college admissions dean and a staff member in charge of transfers expect more insights out of you than they would from a high school student. Of course, since you are older and have gained college experience, you have more insight and that won't be an obstacle. Recommendations should come from professors at your first college, not from your high school teachers. If you have a friend who is a student in the school where you want to go, or if you know a graduate of the college, send him in to meet the transfer admissions officer and put in a good word for you.

Do some research. Find out how many transfers will be allowed to join your class. Ask where you can live. (If you don't yet have friends there, try to live on campus at least the first semester so you can easily and naturally meet a lot of students.) Do they have a new students' orientation for transfer students? Try to visit the campus before you apply. Go to the department where you plan to major, and meet some of the other majors and professors.

In the meantime, carefully check Chapter 3—What's Out There? Researching the Colleges—so that you consider all of your options before you make your next move. Remember: It's your college academic record and your personal statement that will get you in where you want to go. Don't hesitate to get over there, meet the transfer admissions officer, and win his heart!

PART III

A Word to the Wise Parents

CHAPTER 13

A PARENTING CHALLENGE

I know. Parents have very different concerns than their sons and daughters going off to college. Seldom does anyone talk about the trauma of having a child leave home. So intense is the "Where will he get in and where will she go?" question that the dread of losing your child lurks silently in your heart.

And, of course, there are money questions too. Is it going to be worth the price? Am I willing to pay $350,000 for a college as finances collapse all around us if the college isn't even Ivy League? Will my child be safe in those coed dorms, in cars with kids drinking and driving? What's the drug story on campus? Do I have to worry about guns on campus? Will my child be safe in some other part of the country where we don't have any friends or relatives? Does he know what he wants? When does preparing for a career come into the college conversation?

Your son or daughter is leaving home—going off to college—and you want your child to have the very best.

The Private Consultant

Many parents ask, "Should I hire a private college counselor to help with this crucial decision for my child? After all, I want what's best for him."

I would ask you, "Does your son have a college advisor or guidance counselor who handles the college process at school?" If he is in a private school, you can be sure that the school thinks they have the best in college advising. After all, like it or not, their reputation is often built on their college list. If your child is in a public school that has a guidance counselor who deals with all the problems of high school (including curriculum choices, behavior problems, poor grades, relationship problems between teachers and students, teachers and parents, students and parents) students are often shortchanged in college advising. If a college counselor has a load of three hundred seniors or more and doesn't have time for individual attention, then outside help may make sense. In fact, public school guidance counselors often recommend the best consultants in their region.

It is not a dilemma for outsiders to work with overextended guidance counselors in areas where their expertise is needed—and sometimes purchased under contract from the school. The private consultants' efforts can fill a great need when they are able to help students and families who don't have a clue about the college selection process and can't get what they need to know from their schools. If your children go to a high school where nobody has gone out of state to college for the past two years, then you may want to get outside help. You surely will want to take a closer look at Chapter 3—What's Out There?

> ▶▶▶ **THE COLLEGE SELECTION** *process is more than your children choosing where they are going next year—it also provides seniors with an educational opportunity that includes a lot of important developmental tasks that they need in order to grow up enough to leave home.*

We want America's high school teenagers to have the privilege of a good education, strong teachers, and a terrific college counselor who knows what she is doing and has time to work with each senior; but like all things in our imperfect world, we don't always get what we need and want. Moreover, the gap between public and private schools is probably at its widest in their college selection programs.

The college selection process is more than your children choosing where they are going next year—it also provides seniors with an educational opportunity that includes a lot of important developmental tasks that they need in order to grow up enough to leave home. Making decisions about college presents young people with a situation in which they must learn how to distinguish themselves from their peers and then develop strategies that highlight those distinguishing characteristics in writing. This process builds character and teaches seniors a skill they will use throughout their lives.

As an educator, I see the college selection process as an independent study in decision-making, a learning experience that prepares students to choose the environments in which they will be most productive and happy. They can choose from hundreds of different campus cultures, none of which is right for everyone, and all of which are wonderful for someone. It is an independent study in which seniors much choose from their options (the colleges from which they were accepted) and consider those options even when they differ from their family's choices.

> ▶▶▶ **THE COLLEGE SELECTION** *process is an independent study in decision-making*.

But now we must consider what can happen to this developmental task when an outsider is brought into the loop of student, high school, and colleges. How could an independent counselor affect the senior in high school? If a family is willing to spend the money, many will ask, "What harm will it do?"

"What harm will it do" is a question that often arises during the college selection process. What harm will it do to do apply early? What harm will it do to apply to a dream school? What harm will it do to apply to eighteen colleges? The questions are always asked by parents as if they didn't have a downside.

Here is the harm to the student: I have never had a senior come in and announce with pride or empowerment that he now has an educational consultant! Never. In surveying my colleagues on this question, I find students are confused (should I be relieved to have another point of view or worried that my counselor won't like it?), embarrassed (it's their parents' idea), and feel deceitful (they avoid their guidance counselors and college advisors). I first learned that one of my students had a private consultant by reading an article in *New York Magazine*. The point of the article was that the outside consultant surely knows a lot more tricks or can play the angles, such as "apply to Cornell's agriculture college rather than to arts and science," as if the admissions professionals at Cornell were unaware of such "backdoor" admissions subterfuge!

> ▶▶▶ **NO MATTER HOW** *inefficient, busy, or unfriendly the guidance counselor appears to be, seniors must make an effort to turn that relationship around and make a friend of the counselor.*

The harm to the student also occurs when the college counselor feels less responsibility toward the student because someone else is doing the job. Many parents are not aware that the high school advocacy of their child makes a difference in a college's selection of freshmen. The high school college counselor is the one who will be advocating or not advocating, communicating or not communicating with the colleges. A young man from a large public high school in New York City came to see me because he didn't trust his guidance counselor to send anything in on time. He wanted the teachers to give him their recommendations and his transcript to send with his application. That doesn't work. No matter how inefficient, busy, or unfriendly the guidance counselor appears to be, seniors must make an effort to turn that relationship around and make a friend of the counselor.

When college admissions personnel have a question about a senior's performance or application, they do not call the coach, the favorite teacher, or the outside consultant—they call only the high school's college advisor or guidance counselor. Seniors need their high school's advocacy. You need the high school advocacy for your child.

The highest-paid consultant in the world can't get anywhere without the student's high school advocacy.

I asked my colleague at a top boarding school, "Hey, Tommy, what do you say to parents who ask you what you think of them getting an outside college consultant?"

"Good," he replied, "now I won't have to worry about your son."

The greatest harm of the independent counselor, however, is that an outsider sometimes teaches a "beat the system mentality" rather than an educational process of self-assessment, research (studying all of the colleges in order to find the best match), and communication with the colleges (application, essay, interviews, and special portfolios). When the independent consultant and the parents who hire him take control of the process, they also take control *away* from the student just when the developmental task of an adolescent is best empowered by parents letting go. The college selection process is an educational process. A student's work toward creating college options teaches independence, self-reliance, and decision-making skills that build confidence, all of which young people will need when they leave home.

> ▶▶▶ **A STUDENT'S WORK** *toward creating college options teaches independence, self-reliance, and decision-making skills that build confidence, all of which young people will need when they leave home.*

Stepping outside the school system often takes away this educational opportunity for seniors. The college selection process is an adolescent's developmental task for transition from home life to campus life. This process belongs in our schools; its value is educational and personal growth. Moms can't write a note to excuse their sons from it. Dads can't pay someone to do it for their daughters. It's the place where students grow into the job. If you do go for a private consultant, let me caution you: Be sure you work in partnership with your son's or daughter's guidance counselor. Be sure your son knows that the college process is his responsibility, even though he is getting help from a private consultant. Keep in mind that your daughter's high school counselor, not her private counselor, has to be her strongest advocate to win the heart of the college admissions dean.

The difficulty for parents is that they know that the competition for college admissions is increasing. The selection process and the odds for bright, highly qualified high school students to get into America's top colleges are different from when they were applying to college in the seventies and eighties. Chances for admission are more competitive than even two years ago when an older sibling may have applied. They're especially different for students from private schools that were often accepted into the most selective colleges because of tradition. Until the past 15 years, many public school students didn't even aspire to attend the top colleges. Most of those students didn't realize that need-based financial aid was available, thus keeping them from even dreaming that admission to our country's top universities was a real possibility. The thousands of international students who are now coming to America for their higher education must also be added to the equation.

> ▶ ▶ ▶ **IF COLLEGES WERE** *stocks, I'd advise you to sell overvalued Duke and Georgetown; buy undervalued Brandeis, Chicago, and the sister colleges; hold Swarthmore, Harvard, and Bowdoin. Sell Amherst and Williams and buy Carleton.*

Simply put, the fundamental law of supply and demand provides many profit-making opportunities in association with college admissions. SAT coaching, packaging students, selling essays, and hiring college consultants outside of high school—and yes, even the publishing world and books like *Eight First Choices*—adds up to a $3 billion-a-year industry.

To maximize its profits, it is important for this industry to keep the image of a tight market in front of the public by defining "top colleges" as a very select few, rather than trumpeting the reality of the hundreds of excellent colleges available to high school seniors. Parents are led to believe that it is always better to choose Harvard, Princeton, and Stanford over Best State University because of top Ivies' presumably superior educational environment, better alumni connections, and more lucrative on-campus recruiting opportunities. Even though an economist at Princeton and a researcher at the Andrew W. Mellon Foundation found no economic advantage in attending a selective college, and even though the majority of top CEOs surveyed by *Fortune* did not attend an elite college, many parents still opt for the $350,000 investment at the most selective colleges in America.

Even Wall Street parents don't consider overvalue when it comes to where their own daughters and sons go to college. "Now look," I often say to those Wall Street parents, "if colleges were stocks, I'd advise you to sell overvalued Duke and Georgetown; buy undervalued Brandeis, Chicago, and the sister colleges; hold Swarthmore, Harvard, and Bowdoin. Sell Amherst and Williams and buy Carleton." They smile, hold on to everything they know, do almost no research on colleges they don't know, and buy any blue chip college they can get their hands on—no matter what the match is for their child or how globalization is changing our world. Choosing a college has become, and continues to be, big business in America.

Within this moneymaking machinery, opportunities for profit—marketing college admissions to thousands of anxious and fearful parents—have become an entrepreneur's delight. The most visible of the businesses are the test-prep tutors and coaching companies that don't hesitate to promise a 100-point improvement in SAT scores.

The ACT/SAT Scare

Wanting to do what's best for your child sometimes means being sure that he gets into one or more of America's top 10 percent of the colleges, the big three hundred. For some of you, it means the big fifty. Still other parents have in mind only the big three: Harvard, Princeton, and Yale. It may sound scary at first to learn that Princeton turns down 76 percent of its applicants who scored between 34/750 and a perfect 36/800 on the ACT/SAT. Following right after these test scores is this revealing statistic: Princeton offered admission to 495 of 1,534 class valedictorians. Think of it. More than one thousand applicants who were number one in the high school class were sent a denial letter from Princeton. But on second thought, isn't it encouraging and refreshing to realize that your child doesn't need a perfect score and perfect grades to get in? Isn't it good to know that numbers alone won't do it?

▶▶▶ **THERE ISN'T A** *college in the country where a motivated student with ACT/SAT scores of 29/680-680 critical reading and math can't do the work.*

When you begin to realize that it's true—that numbers alone won't get him or her in—then you realize that your son and daughter can concentrate on learning and doing interesting things that are unique to them rather than spending two years of Saturdays at a test-prep course. For example, they could be reading instead of memorizing vocabulary from flash cards. Or the teenagers at your house could be involved in the school play or practicing cello or collecting model World War II tanks. Your children can develop their interests and skills and sensibilities, rather than attempting to mold themselves into testing robots. And keep in mind that test robot results won't necessarily get them where their SATs promise.

Test scores disappoint! The numbers (ACT/SAT scores and grades) your children achieve could get them into the top colleges if deans and admissions committees were looking only at the qualifications necessary to do the work at a particular college. But they're not looking only at Allison's or Paul's ability to do the work. As parents, teachers, and counselors, that may be what we see. But it's not what the colleges will assess.

College personnel review thousands of applications, known as the "applicant pool," for a few hundred freshman places. They separate out interesting young people for their freshman community who are within a wide test-score range. Colleges want more than test robots. They want to know that students have the ability to *use* their mental gifts, to apply their reasoning skills in a variety of ways. It's not just the test scores that speak to the college deans, but what students can do—and what they choose to do—with the brainpower behind those raw high numbers.

There isn't a college in the country where a motivated student with ACT/SAT scores of 29/680 critical reading and math can't do the work. The last thing a college admissions dean does is compare Jane with Dick and say, "Oh, these two are exactly alike except Jane is thirty points higher on her reading, so we will take her." Yet many of the questions to college admissions deans run as if this is the basic assumption of students and their parents.

A Colgate college admissions dean once told me, "After we select the qualified applicants out, we still have thousands of applications for five hundred places. Then we make a selective judgment of just what kind of brain the kid has. How does she think? What kind of a learner is he? We look for the student who can ask the best questions, not the one who knows only the right answers."

The Dean's Point of View

To help us make sense of the competition for college admission, let's look from the admissions dean's point of view and try to understand what selection committees search for. When I asked Harvard's Dean Fitzsimmons what he is after—what he looks at most closely—he just nodded his head as if that were the wrong question and told me, "Everything. We look at everything." That means that once a student is within a reasonable range of curriculum, grades, and SATs, the admissions dean is looking for someone who can be a contributing member of an interesting freshman class and who will be a perfect match for his particular campus culture. They consider curriculum choice; in-depth study, especially in mathematics, foreign language, and science; and the risk-taking factor, especially in areas the student isn't crazy about. As the deans read through the folders, many students just pop right up as instant superstars and fascinating applicants.

Why some applications and not others? It isn't so much "What's wrong with an application?" as it is a matter of what's right with the outstanding ones. Let me explain. Think of what it takes to be a champion athlete. Let's take a track star or swimmer. We can measure the numbers—height, weight, time, speed, and distance of previous events—but what we look for in a winner is also motivation, discipline, coachability, attitude about winning, ability to focus in all kinds of weather, and ability to function with tight competition on his or her heels. Numbers alone don't do it. Values, attitudes, and behavior have to be factored into the decision—and they are.

▶▶▶ **IF THE TOP** *colleges value one skill above all others, it is writing.*

If the top colleges value one skill above all others, it is writing. Doesn't that make sense? After all, writing reflects how one thinks and can express oneself. Good writing means more than something being deemed technically correct. An essay can be correct and very ordinary. Most writing is. Most people are. It's the extraordinary writer that the selective colleges are looking for—that student whose written word soars, or is inspirational or logical within a different system of reasoning from the ordinary, or creative and innovative in how students see themselves in the world. A teacher can encourage all of these qualities, but it is within the young person's experience that a few shine and stand out above all others. These are the select human beings from all over the world that get to go to the top of the top colleges. Their range of ACT/SAT scores will vary from 29/680 reading to 36/800. A few will come in under that.

What else are the colleges looking for? Besides finding the fascinating, curious, smart student, colleges need to fill the positions that will provide leadership for the college community. As a director of admissions responding to this question put it, "If I need a quarterback, I'm going to get one!" Besides quarterbacks, those roles will be filled in a variety of areas, including all of the institution's priorities: legacies; publications, student government, racial and gender balance; children of influential and donor families; athletic teams and music groups. The admissions staff also has to come up with the diversity that can only be provided by underrepresented ethnic, language, and international groups the world over.

America's top colleges get to choose their freshmen from thousands of interesting young people who will eventually lead the world in every imaginable field. Their abilities and sensibilities develop through opportunities they find in their family and high school communities. How high school students spend their time outside the classroom is the measure of their values. The selective college applicants are curious, disciplined young people who have already made a mark in filmmaking, Olympic athletics, international church work, publishing software programs, regional political contests, poetry readings, university science labs, Broadway roles, and country-western music composition. Spending their school years distinguishing themselves and documenting their achievement in essay form is what will get your children where you wish they could go.

Family Life Is Hard to Do

Letting your child make the final college choice is often a frustrating task. Some of the difficulty is that you would do things differently, were it your decision. It's hard to keep a balance of doing it your way and encouraging your children to do it their way. Here are some ideas that might help your family cope.

Open Minds Win

In this highly competitive world, the first thing a teenager's parents should to do in order to understand the college admissions system is to broaden their own knowledge concerning the hundreds of excellent colleges and universities from which your children may choose. Research colleges right along with your son or daughter by reading *The Ultimate Guide to America's Best Colleges* and *The Fiske Guide to Colleges.* This will get you started so that you have an overview of what is out there. Try hard to keep an open mind and help your child to do the same. Don't get stuck on "She has to go to Brown." I just can't begin to tell you how many terribly disappointed and distraught parents in April come back at Christmastime of the following year to say, "What a wonderful match Susie Q. has found at Elon or Grinnell. We are on the parent committee and let me tell you about their outreach to high schools."

Downplay the hysteria in the media—the front-page SAT stories. Focus on the process your son is going through, encouraging him as he discovers what he wants and learns how he can get it. Try to keep your daughter's mind open as she researches colleges. This responsibility is harder to do than it sounds. We all hear so much about a very few of the terrific colleges and universities in America. And we can't help but think that if we know about a certain school, it must be better than one we've never heard of—after all, that's what marketing and advertising is all about! But when parents become aware of the process, many can get beyond the college name and ranking. They too start to ask, "What's it like? What's the fit? What is the outlook for my son and daughter if they go to your school?"

Write a Letter to the Guidance Counselor

Here's an opportunity to give your input about your daughter; a chance to say what she's like to live with at home and how she relates to her brothers and sisters, family pet, grandparents, and neighbors; a place for you to write about her special talents, her cares and worries. Some parents have written about childhood illness, unusual emotional stress in the family (more than the regular stress that we all have), rational for poor grades, high hopes, responsibilities children take on in the home.

Write anything that will add a family dimension to the counselor's understanding of a student. It helps the school counselor be an advocate for your child because she can use what she has learned from you in her recommendation to the colleges. Parent letters are invaluable for student descriptions. A letter to the guidance counselor is your chance to get your message across to the college admissions dean about how unique your son or daughter really is. Tell a story or relate an incident. Tell how he has overcome disappointments and what you're most proud of.

Even though the counselor may not ask for a written description of your son or daughter, any counselor in the country who has to get those student recommendation letters written before November 1 and January 1 can use a parent's written statement to better describe her students. I'm going to trust that you are smart enough not to tell the counselor how to do her job and that you'll think of a natural way to get your letter to her. Remember that this counselor is your child's advocate. The better she knows him or her, the stronger her advocacy will be. So with your best smile, in your most off-hand manner, offer the letter with an "in case you find it helpful" kind of phrase.

Here is a parent questionnaire that a boarding school asks their parents to fill out before they meet for a college conference. This may give you some helpful ideas of what to include in a letter to your child's guidance counselor.

> ➤ What characteristics are you especially interested in finding in a college for your son or daughter?

> ➤ List three adjectives which describe your son or daughter.

> ➤ Describe your child—her "learning style," motivation, strengths, areas needing improvement. What are her principal achievements?

> ➤ I am proud of my child because . . .

> ➤ Are there any family situations, medical history, special awards that we should know about which would be helpful in describing him?

> ➤ Will your child be applying for financial aid?

> ➤ How important is college prestige in your support of your child's college choice?

> ➤ How do you see your child distinguishing himself from his siblings or friends? In what ways is she her own person?

If you aren't comfortable with a letter, write an outline. Tell what you most admire about your child. Describe what you like most about living with him. Write everything you wish the college knew about your daughter or son! If you don't have a college conference with the guidance counselor, then it's all the more important to get in your two cents' worth. Remember that the unconscious mind is always at work in winning a heart, and we all like best what we know best. Be sure that the counselor knows your son and daughter best. Don't drive them crazy with information they don't want, but one letter or outline describing your child can't possibly be interpreted as too much.

The College Process Builds Character

You've heard it before and you know how important it is that your daughter and son feel free to make their own college decisions in order to gain a sense of responsibility and independence. After all, they are the ones who are going to be living the consequences of their choices for four years. The college selection process is tough. It builds character. And heaven knows that students will need character to succeed in their first year away from home—that first year at college.

Blessed Assurance

No matter how good you are at parenting, it's hard not to feel overwhelmed with anxiety in late March of your child's senior year. Talking to your school guidance counselor, principal, or headmaster just doesn't help for long. In fact, no one else can help because the only thing that will lessen that anxiety is the college decision letter. I tell my parents to try to change the subject in their heads—exercise, go out and run or ski or just plain walk fast. Whatever your coping mechanism is for high anxiety, get that coping machinery well oiled and in place before February and March, because every parent of a high school senior in the college selection process needs it. A sense of humor and perspective helps too, but in the college-panic months of February and March, logical solutions let us down—humor goes out the window and perspective pulls the shade. The hard truth is that blessed assurance will not be yours until the fat letter that sings a YES arrives in your mail. In the meantime, help your son and daughter by simply believing in them. At least, acting as if you do.

COLLEGE ADMISSIONS TALK

College admissions has its own language. Here are some terms you should know.

Advanced Placement (AP): College-level courses offered in high school for which students may earn college credit. Students can qualify for advanced standing when they enroll in college; students may take the AP Exams in May whether they have taken the course or not.

American College Test (ACT): A college entrance test administered by the American College Testing Corporation. Most colleges allow students to submit scores from either the ACT or SAT. Parents often wonder if their children score better on the ACT or the SAT. Check the chapter on College Admissions Testing to think about which is best for your child.

Arts and sciences (the liberal arts): This is the college within a university, or a separate college course of study, that includes the humanities, social sciences, natural sciences, mathematics, foreign languages, and fine arts. It's America's typical undergraduate college.

Block system: The academic year is divided into nine three-and-one-half-week blocks. A student takes only one course at a time, total immersion, which gives no excuses for "I have to do the other subject first." The block system appears to be a procrastinator's hell. There are no excuses. It also permits the courses to be held off campus. Colorado College has made the block system famous.

Candidates' reply date: The May 1 deadline, observed by the selective colleges by which the applicant must respond to one offer of admission, usually with a deposit. As the competition gets more fierce, the colleges apply the rules concerning the May 1 deposit more rigorously.

Coalition Application: The latest of three online college applications accepted by about 70 colleges. Allows space to collect four years of high school work to use when applying to college in senior year.

College Board: Administers the PSAT, the SAT, the SAT Subject Test, the Advanced Placement (AP) tests, the College Scholarship Service (CSS), and PROFILE. The SATs are developed in arrangement with the Educational Testing Service (ETS).

Common Application: One of three online multiple college application forms accepted by about 900 colleges. The Common App is often supplemented by the college's own form. It is available online at www.commonapp.org.

Comprehensive exams: Final tests given college seniors in some selective liberal arts colleges, usually in their major; often required to graduate.

Consortium: A group of colleges and universities that offer joint programs, cross-registration for academic course work, and coordinated social, cultural, and athletic programs to the students within the affiliated group. For example: Amherst, Hampshire, the University of Massachusetts, Mount Holyoke, and Smith are the Five College Consortium.

Core curriculum: A specified program of required courses that all students must take in order to graduate.

CSS (College Scholarship Service) PROFILE: A financial aid form from the College Board that is required by many of the selective private colleges and universities for students seeking financial aid in addition to the national FAFSA.

Deferral: Postponement of applicants for early decision or early action that will be considered within the regular applicant pool. Also a postponement for some students from the waitlist to defer until the next January, February, or even for a year. Some students request a deferral after being admitted in order to take a Gap Year program.

Distribution requirements: Required courses for college graduation. Usually a student can choose from many courses within the categories of the humanities, social sciences, sciences, fine arts, foreign languages, and mathematics.

Demonstrated need: The difference between the family contribution as established on the Expected Family Contribution (EFC) and the total cost of attending the college.

Early Action (EA): A program whereby students receive an early admission, deferral, or denial decision in December, but are not obligated to enroll if admitted. Harvard, Princeton, Yale and Stanford are best known for "single-choice" or "restricted" (REA); other well-known schools with EA programs include Boston College, Chicago, Georgetown, MIT, and Notre Dame. A May 1 response is required.

Early Decision (ED): A program whereby students apply by the first or middle of November and receive an early admission, deferral, or denial decision in December, and are obligated to enroll if admitted and if financial aid award is sufficient. If admitted, ED students are required to withdraw all other college applications. Increasingly colleges are offering a second or "late" early decision, with decisions given in February; some even offer a "late-late" ED.

ETS: Education Testing Service, Princeton, NJ; develops college entrance tests for the College Board.

Expected Family Contribution (EFC): The amount that a family is expected to pay for one year of college as determined by standardized forms from FAFSA or PROFILE.

FAFSA: See Free Application for Federal Student Aid.

Federal methodology (FM): The method of calculating the Expected Family Contribution (EFC) that is determined only on the FAFSA and the federal aid formula.

Fee waiver: Exemptions for needy students to apply for college admission without having to pay the application fee, for the SAT, the SAT Subject Tests, and for the PROFILE.

FFS: Family Financial Statement from ACT.

Financial aid package: The combination of aid awarded by a college that may include grants, loans, and a work-study job.

Four-one-four: An academic calendar consisting of two regular four-month semesters with a short winter or January term in between.

Free Application for Federal Student Aid (FAFSA): A financial aid form produced by the federal government that is required by nearly all colleges and universities for students seeking aid, loans, or work-study jobs.

Gapping: The practice of offering less financial aid than the student's calculated need.

Gap Year: Usually a year off from school between high school graduation and first year of college. Check out the American Gap Association website to learn how, why, where, and when.

Graduate student: A college student who has completed the bachelor's degree and is working toward a master's or doctoral degree.

Greek system: Fraternities and sororities on campus. They are called "Greek" because their names originate from letters in the Greek alphabet.

Humanities: Courses in which the primary focus is on human culture; this includes philosophy, foreign language, religion, and literature.

Institutional methodology (IM): A method of calculating Expected Family Contribution (EFC) that includes the FAFSA and the college's own financial aid form and takes into consideration the institution's priorities.

Interdisciplinary major: Combined majors such as political science, philosophy, and economics, or Spanish and business administration, often created and negotiated by students.

International Baccalaureate (IB): A precisely prescribed high school program originated in Geneva, Switzerland, which is available around the world. Americans can earn advanced standing in American colleges, and many fulfill the thirteenth year requirement of foreign universities.

Language requirement: A foreign language graduation requirement at many colleges. Most AP students are exempt from this requirement if their scores meet the standard of the college. Many others can place out of the requirement through examinations during freshman orientation week.

Legacy: An applicant whose parents or grandparents are graduates of a particular college. Siblings, uncles, and aunts are not usually considered legacy. Most colleges give academically qualified legacies an edge in admissions.

Liberal arts college: The college within a university or a separate college course of study that includes the humanities, social sciences, natural sciences, mathematics, foreign languages, and fine arts. It's America's typical undergraduate college.

Merit scholarship: A financial grant for college awarded on academic achievement or special skill and talent in an extracurricular activity in high school. Merit scholarships are not awarded based on need. Unrelated to the National Merit Scholarship Program.

National Merit Scholarship Program: A scholarship program that begins with the scores on the Preliminary SAT (PSAT) taken in October of the junior year. Separate programs award black and Hispanic students from the same PSAT exam.

Need-blind admissions: A policy in which the applicant's ability to pay for college does not affect the admissions decision. Fewer and fewer colleges subscribe to this policy.

Open admissions: A policy whereby any student with a high school diploma is accepted, usually a policy of public universities for resident students.

Parietals: Rules that govern times when students of one sex may visit dorms or floors housing the opposite sex. Out-of-fashion rule at most, but not all, colleges.

Pass-fail: An option to replace grades at some colleges to encourage students to take courses outside their major interests and talents, and an option at some colleges for first semester of freshman year.

Preliminary SAT (PSAT): A qualifying test for the National Merit Scholarship Program from the College Board, administered in October of junior year, and often offered to tenth graders as a practice test.

Preferential packaging: A policy of awarding financial aid in which colleges offer the best aid to their most desired applicants.

PROFILE: A financial aid form from the College Board that is required by many of the selective private colleges and universities for students seeking financial aid.

PSAT: See Preliminary SAT.

Restricted Early Action (REA): Harvard, Princeton, Yale, and Stanford are best known for "single-choice" or "restricted" Early Action. Other well-known schools with EA programs include Boston College, Georgetown, MIT, Notre Dame, and Wellesley. Students agree not to apply to any other Early programs of a private university, but may apply Regular decision to all other universities, and may apply early to state universities. A May 1 response is required.

Quad: An abbreviation of "quadrangle" found on many traditional campuses, where the classroom or dorm complexes are built on a square or rectangle with a green in the center.

Quarter system: An academic calendar of four quarters, of which three constitute a full academic year; sometimes called the Dartmouth Plan, where students must attend one summer in the four years. This system encourages students to be more creative in their off-campus time, which can come any time of year, not only in the summer.

Resident advisor (RA): A paid student personnel officer or an upper-classman living in a freshman dorm to offer support and advice to new students.

Residential college: A living unit within a larger institution that offers special academic programs to its students; best models at Rice and Yale. In public universities, a residential college is also called a living/learning community.

Restricted Early Action (REA): Boston College, Georgetown, Harvard, MIT, Notre Dame, Princeton, Stanford, and Yale, are "single-choice" or "restricted" Early Action. Students agree not to apply to any other Early programs of a private university, but may apply Regular decision to all other universities, and may apply early to state universities. A May 1 response is required.

Rolling admissions: An admissions policy by which a college evaluates and decides upon applicants as soon as the application is complete. Colleges often promise a decision within six weeks. Public universities are often rolling, although they can hold places until April for out-of-state students, and the dates tend to vary each year.

SAR: See Student Aid Report.

SAT and SAT Subject Test: The most widely used college entrance examinations (2.22 million test-takers in 2020) administered by the College Board and created by Educational Testing Service (ETS). The SAT: Reasoning Test is a three hour test that measures critical reading and math logic. The SAT Subject Tests are one-hour tests measuring achievement in a particular course of study.

Score Choice: An option whereby students can choose which SAT and SAT Subject Test scores they want to send to the colleges.

Semester system: Two blocks of several months each, constituting a full academic year at most American colleges. Students take summers off.

Social sciences: College courses that deal with human society, including anthropology, economics, history, political science, psychology, and sociology.

Student Aid Report (SAR): The form sent to families after filing their FAFSA form that tells the student the Expected Family Contribution (EFC).

Teaching assistant (TA): A graduate student who teaches undergraduates, and/or holds smaller discussion sections or study groups in conjunction with a professor's lectures.

Three-two program (3-2): A program in which students study three years in a liberal arts college followed by two years at a specialized school. Examples are engineering, nursing, or business administration.

Trimesters: The academic calendar divided into three equal terms to constitute a full year.

Undergraduate: A college student working toward a bachelor's degree; usually a four-year program.

Universal Application: One of three multiple online apps, it represents around 35 colleges.

Waitlist: The list of students who are qualified to attend but not yet accepted. Also called late decision by the author, many students get into the college they most want to attend from the waitlist. It is also used for political reasons, so that the dean of admissions doesn't have to deny a legacy or donor family.

Work-study: A federally funded program whereby students are given campus jobs as part of their financial package. Students must fill out the FAFSA form in order to get a work-study position.

Yield: The percentage of the accepted students who enrolled at a particular college. Some say that admissions are driven by yield, because colleges are often rated by how many students enroll from the accepted list.

ANNOTATED RESOURCES

Books

Eight First Choices: An Expert's Strategies for Getting into College, Fourth Edition, by Joyce Slayton Mitchell (SuperCollege). Also in Ebook. Do you want to know how to get started and stay on track for the college selection process? Want to know how to research what's out there among the 2,400 U.S. colleges? Do you want tips on how to write the application and essay? And short questions? Do you want to know which tests to take when? How to negotiate the interview and find out about financial aid? Then read *Eight First Choices*, fourth edition, the college admissions book endorsed by more college admissions deans than any other college guide on the market.

Who is This Kid? Colleges Want to Know! Writing Exercises for Winning Applications, by Joyce Slayton Mitchell (Critical Thinking Co.) Who is this kid? That's what the college deans of admissions want to know. Self-assessment writing exercises, with communications and how to research your choices skills, students will learn how to separate themselves from the hundreds of other American and international students applying to the same competitive colleges. Ebook also available online from Amazon and www.criticalthinking.com/who-is-this-kid-book.

Campus Culture: What's My Match? By Joyce Slayton Mitchell (Ebook). Going beyond the rankings, majors, locations, and the advice that high school students hear from everyone, *College Culture: What's My Match?* considers the kind of student life that feels right for the particular student. The principle of the book is based on the philosophy that every college is wonderful for someone. No college is great for everyone. Ebook available online from iTunes, Amazon, and Barnes & Noble.

The Chinese Guide to American Colleges, by Joyce Slayton Mitchell, Ebook on Apple, Amazon, and Barnes & Noble. The one and only guide written in Mandarin for Chinese students and their parents with everything you need to know to research U.S. colleges and universities with a list of the top 150. How to write the essay and application, which tests to take when, everything you need to know to apply to American colleges!

The Indian Guide to American Colleges, by Joyce Slayton Mitchell, Ebook on Apple, Amazon, and Barnes & Noble, 2012. Print edition, Hay House. The one and only guide written for Indian students and their parents with everything you need to know to research U.S. colleges and universities with a list of the top 150. How to write the essay and application, which tests to take when, everything you need to know to apply to American colleges!

The Korean Guide to American Colleges, by Joyce Slayton Mitchell, Ebook on Apple, Amazon, and Barnes & Noble, in press – November, 2012. The one and only complete guide written only for Korean students and their parents with everything you need to know to research U.S. colleges and universities with a list of the top 150. How to write the essay and application, which tests to take when, everything you need to know to apply to American colleges!

The Vietnamese Guide to American Colleges, by Joyce Slayton Mitchell, Ebook on Apple, Amazon, and Barnes & Noble, 2012. The one and only guide written for Vietnamese students and their parents with everything you need to know to research U.S. colleges and universities with a list of the top 150. How to write the essay and application, which tests to take when, everything you need to know to apply to American colleges!

The Ultimate Guide to America's Best Colleges, latest edition (SuperCollege). The only guidebook of its kind to combine extensive narrative college profiles with detailed data and statistics on each institution, this tome reports on more than 300 colleges and universities, addressing their academics, majors, student life, athletics, student body, distinguished alumni, admissions, financial aid, and postgraduation success. Tips on each college's admission process and student quotes from a national survey accompany each description to provide an honest and thorough appraisal of each college's strengths and weaknesses. To guide students by the numbers, this book includes extensive statistics for each school, with figures on the student composition, class sizes, most popular majors, admissions rates, required standardized tests, deadlines, college costs, and financial aid. A must-have, go-to resource for any college-bound student, their parents, or guidance and career counselors, readers will also find a ranking of the 100 best college values.

The combination of these few selected guides are worth 20 visits to the college campus. Be sure to get an idea of "what it's like" to be on campus. Again, about 350 colleges are described—the top 10 percent of U.S. colleges. Some of the data from *Insider's* is specific and not easily found anywhere else. Read the guides for percent of public school students, percent in fraternities, numbers of transfers, most popular majors (not best, but most popular), percent of students living on campus, retention rate (the percentage of students who stay for sophomore year). All the college websites are listed.

The Fiske Guide to Colleges, latest edition, by Edward B. Fiske (Random House). This book boasts the best campus descriptions of about 350 colleges. Don't take the ratings and SAT scores needed to get in too seriously. It's the three-page description of each college that is crucial for you to study in order to have an overall understanding of what's out there in American higher education. The guide describes the college's strongest departments and majors, the quality of academic and social life, and it gives you websites and email addresses.

You will also want to look carefully at *Fiske's* "overlaps." Those are the other colleges and universities to which a particular college's applicants are also applying in greatest numbers. These schools represent its major competition. For example, if one of your choices is Wisconsin's Beloit College, then you will see that two of the overlaps are Ripon and Lawrence, both of which have many of the same qualities. Check 'em out! If Bucknell seems like a terrific match for you, then check out *Fiske's* overlaps and you will find Lafayette, Lehigh, and Penn State. Although Penn State is a state university and much bigger, it has qualities (geography has to be one of them!) that attract similar applicants. One more: Let's say you've checked it out and you are crazy about Notre Dame. Looking at the overlaps, you will find two other Catholic universities, Boston College and Georgetown; you will also find Duke, Northwestern, and Michigan.

The College Handbook, latest edition (The College Board). This is one of the most accurate and up-to-date "big" college guides available. The College Board collects the data, including which SAT tests are required by each college, each year from their own membership. Every college in the country is in this guide. *Fiske* and *Insider's* describe 10 percent of the most selective and interesting colleges in America. Those 350 colleges, along with the other 90 percent of American colleges, will be cited in *The College Handbook*. Be sure to read the Student Life section, and if you plan to be a residential student, check out the percentage of students living in the dorms.

Paying for College Without Going Broke, by Kalman A. Chany (Princeton Review, annual). Kal Chany is the financial planning guru who knows where to put your money to get the best value out of your college dollar. Written by a big-time New Yorker who knows college finance well, this book is packed with good advice on the latest changes and which forms to fill out when and which format to use. You'll find up-to-date nuts and bolts instructions that will help you wade through the many financial aid forms.

International Student Handbook (The College Board, latest edition). This is the best official guide for international students. It is written in cooperation among the College Board's Office of International Education, U.S. government agencies involved with international educational exchange, overseas educational advisors, and international admission officers at U.S. colleges. Everything international students need to know about ESL programs, TOEFL scores, international testing centers, application deadlines, financial aid, and housing can be found on the pages of this handbook. It also offers a complete worldwide list of international advising centers.

Web Sites

ACT Examinations: www.actstudent.org. You can register for the ACTs, check the schedule, fees, colleges accepting the ACT exam, and find answers to your college admissions testing questions.

American Gap Association: http://www.americangap.org. Programs for high school and college students with U.S. and international opportunities to travel, study, intern, work, and more.

Art Students: www.allartschools.com. Check out this site for performing and visual arts schools, portfolio information, and special arts programs.

Black students: www.blackexcel.org. Learn about the latest scholarships, SAT requirements, and racial issues in college admissions from this Web site, recommended highly by *Ebony* and *Black Enterprise*.

Coalition Application: www.coalitionforcollegeaccess.org

College Board: www.collegeboard.com. You can register for the SATs, download the CSS PROFILE financial aid form, do a college search, a scholarship search, ask questions and find test preparation online.

College Edge: www.collegedge.com . Besides offering a college search, this site also includes a scholarship search.

Common Application: www.commomapp.org. Original online app for multiple applications covering about 700 colleges.

Educational Testing Service: www.ets.org. Get the SAT and TOEFL test dates as well as practice questions that you need for studying. Register for these tests through the College Board Web site.

Financial-aid site: www.finaid.org. Consider this the best site for all of your financial-aid questions. It is a nonprofit site developed by college financial aid professionals.

Financial: Applying for Aid: http://campusconsultants.com

Free Application for Federal Student Aid (FAFSA) form: www.fafsa.ed.gov. Every college requires this form for student aid and work-study programs.

IELTS: Online: www.ielts.org. Register, then check out the test centers and American Universities that accept the ISELTS for admission.

Joyce Slayton Mitchell: www.JoyceSlaytonMitchell.com, the author's website with free papers for all aspects of the college counseling process.

LGBT students: Award-winning LGBT news site, sponsor of the Advocate college guide: www.advocate.com.

Optional SAT and ACT college admissions tests: www.fairtest.org.

Princeton Review: www.review.com. Look here to find a college search program.

PROFILE form: www.collegeboard.com

Savingforcollege.com: Details on each state's program for college saving plans and chart to compare costs of different plans are included.

TOEFL Online: www.toefl.org. Register, find out the test dates, and get practice questions online.

United States Department of Education: www.ed.gov. Request The Student Guide: Financial Aid from the U.S. Department of Education and your FAFSA form.

Universal Application: www.universalcollegeapp.com

U.S. News and World Report: www.usnews.com. Learn how colleges are rated and find what is important to you.

TOP 101 AMERICAN COLLEGES

Amherst College, Amherst, MA 01002 www.amherst.edu

Bard College, Annandale-on-Hudson, NY 12504 www.bard.edu

Barnard College, New York, NY 10027 www.barnard.edu

Bates College, Lewiston, ME 04240 www.bates.edu

Beloit College, Beloit, WI 53511 www.beloit.edu

Berkeley, University of California at, Berkeley, CA 94720 www.berkeley.edu

Boston College, Chestnut Hill, MA 02467 www.bc.edu

Bowdoin College, Brunswick, ME 04011 www.bowdoin.edu

Brandeis, Waltham, MA 02454 www.brandeis.edu

Brown University, Providence, RI 02912 www.brown.edu

Bryn Mawr College, Bryn Mawr, PA l90l0 www.brynmawr.edu

Bucknell University, Lewisburg PA 17837 www.bucknell.edu

California Institute of Technology, Pasadena, CA 91125 www.caltech.edu

Carleton College, Northfield, MN 55057 www.carleton.edu

Carnegie Mellon University, Pittsburgh, PA 15213 www.cmu.edu

Case Western Reserve University, Cleveland, OH 44106 www.cwru.edu

Centre College, Danville, KY 40422 www.centre.edu

Chicago, University of, Chicago, IL www.chicago.edu

Claremont McKenna College, Claremont, CA 91711 www.mckenna.edu

Colby College, Waterville, ME 04901 www.colby.edu

Colgate University, Hamilton, NY 13346 www.colgate.edu

Colorado College, Colorado Springs, CO 80903 www.coloradocollege.edu

Columbia University, New York, NY 10027 www.columbia.edu

Connecticut College, New London, CT 06320 www.conncoll.edu

Cooper Union, New York, NY 10003 www.cooper.edu

Cornell University, Ithaca, NY 14850 www.cornell.edu

Dartmouth College, Hanover, NH 03755 www.dartmouth.edu

Davidson College, Davidson, NC 28036 www.davidson.edu

Denison University, Granville, OH 43023 www.denison.edu

Dickinson College, Carlisle, PA 17013 www.dickinson.edu

Duke University, Durham, NC 27708 www.duke.edu

Elon University, Elon, NC 27244 www.elon.edu

Emory University, Atlanta, GA 30322 www.emory.edu

Evergreen State University, Olympia, WA 98505 www.evergreen.edu

Franklin and Marshall College, Lancaster, PA 17604 www.fandm.edu

Georgetown University, Washington, DC 20057 www.georgetowncollege.edu

Georgia Institute of Technology, Atlanta, GA 30332 www.gatech.edu

Goucher College, Baltimore, MD 21204 www.goucher.edu

Grinnell College, Grinnell, IA 50112 www.grinnell.edu

Hamilton College, Clinton, NY 13323 www.hamilton.edu

Harvard University, Cambridge, MA 02138 www.harvard.edu

Harvey Mudd College, Claremont, CA 91711 www.hmc.edu

Haverford College, Haverford, PA 19041 www.haverford.edu

Holy Cross, College of the, Worcester, MA 01610 www.holycross.edu

Indiana University, Bloomington, IN 47405 www.iub.edu

Johns Hopkins University, Baltimore, MD 21218 www.jhu.edu

Kenyon College, Gambier, OH 43022 www.kenyon.edu

Lafayette College, Easton, PA 18042 www.lafayette.edu

Lehigh University, Bethlehem, PA 18015 www.lehigh.edu

Lewis and Clark College, Portland, OR 97210 www.clark.edu

Los Angeles, University of California at (UCLA), Los Angeles, CA 90095 www.ucla.edu

Lynn University, Boca Raton, FL 33431 www.lynn.edu

Macalester College, St. Paul, MN 55105 www.macalester.edu

Maryland, University of, College Park, MD 20742 www.umd.edu

Massachusetts Institute of Technology, Cambridge, MA 02139 www.mit.edu

Michigan, University of, Ann Arbor, MI 33124 www.umich.edu

Middlebury College, Middlebury, VT 05753 www.middlebury.edu

Mount Holyoke College, South Hadley, MA 01075 www.mtholyoke.edu

New York University, New York, NY 10012 www.nyu.edu

North Carolina at Chapel Hill, University of, Chapel Hill, NC 25799 www.unc.edu

Northwestern University, Evanston, IL 60208 www.nwu.edu

Notre Dame, University of, Notre Dame, IN 46556 www.nd.edu

Oberlin College, Oberlin, OH 44074 www.oberlin.edu

Occidental College, Los Angeles, CA 90041 www.oxy.edu

Pennsylvania, University of, Philadelphia, PA 19104 www.upenn.edu

Pitzer College, Claremont, CA 91711 www.pitzer.edu

Pomona College, Claremont, CA 91711 www.pomona.edu

Princeton University, Princeton, NJ 08544 www.princeton.edu

Reed College, Portland, OR 97202 www.reed.edu

Rensselaer Polytechnic Institute, Troy, NY 12180 www.rpi.edu

Rhodes College, Memphis, TN 38112 www.rhodes.edu

Rice University, Houston, TX 77005 www.rice.edu

Rochester, University of, Rochester, NY 15627 www.rochester.edu

Rutgers University, Brunswick, NJ 08901 www.rutgers.edu

St. John's College, Annapolis, MD 21402 www.sjca.edu; and Santa Fe, NM 87501 www.sjcsf.edu

San Diego, University of California at, La Jolla, CA 92093 www.ucsd.edu

Santa Clara University, Santa Clara, CA 95053 www.scu.edu

Santa Cruz, University of California at, Santa Cruz, CA 95064 www.ucsc.edu

Scripps College, Claremont, CA 91711 www.scrippscol.edu

Skidmore College, Saratoga Springs, NY 12866 www.skidmore.edu

Smith College, Northampton, MA 01063 www.smith.edu

Stanford University, Stanford, CA 94305 www.stanford.edu

SUNY, Binghamton, Binghamton, NY 13902 www.binghamton.edu

Swarthmore College, Swarthmore, PA 19081 www.swarthmore.edu

Syracuse University, Syracuse, NY 13244 www.syr.edu

Texas, University of, Austin, TX 78712 www.utexas.edu

Trinity College, Hartford, CT 06106 www.trincoll.edu

Tufts University, Medford, MA 02155 www.tufts.edu

Tulane University, New Orleans, LA 70118 www.tulane.edu

Union College, Schenectady, NY 12308 www.union.edu

Vanderbilt University, Nashville, TN 37240 www.vanderbilt.edu

Vassar College, Poughkeepsie, NY 12604 www.vassar.edu

Vermont, University of, Burlington, VT 05405 www.uvm.edu

Virginia, University of, Charlottesville, VA 22904 www.virginia.edu

Wake Forest University, Winston-Salem, NC 27106 www.wfu.edu

Washington and Lee University, Lexington, VA 24450 www.wlu.edu

Washington University, St. Louis, MO 93130 www.wustl.edu

Wellesley College, Wellesley, MA 02481 www.wellesley.edu

Wesleyan University, Middletown, CT 06457 www.wesleyan.edu

Whitman College, Walla Walla, WA 99362 www.whitman.edu

William and Mary, College of, Williamsburg, VA 23187 www.wm.edu

Williams College, Williamstown, MA 01267 www.williams.edu

Wisconsin, University of, Madison, WI 53706 www.wisc.edu

Yale University, New Haven, CT 06520 www.yale.edu

Yeshiva University, New York, NY 10033 www.yu.edu

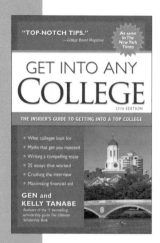

LEARN HOW TO GET INTO
THE COLLEGE OF YOUR DREAMS

- A complete, step-by-step guide to acing college applications, essays, interviews and more

- How to get free cash for college

- Tips for 9th-12th graders

- How to raise your SAT and ACT scores

- Secrets to writing an irresistible essay

- How to create a stunning application

- Tips for mastering the interview

- Proven methods for parents to give your student an edge

Get into Any College

ISBN13: 978-1-61760-160-6

Price: $17.99

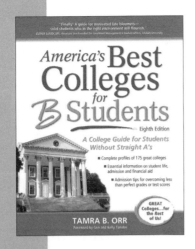

AMERICA'S BEST COLLEGES FOR B STUDENTS: A COLLEGE GUIDE FOR STUDENTS WITHOUT STRAIGHT A'S

- Complete profiles of 175 great colleges that welcome students like you

- Information on academics, majors and what the colleges seek

- Admission tips for overcoming less than perfect grades or test scores

- Inside advice from students, counselors and admission officers

America's Best Colleges for B Students

ISBN: 978-1-61760-151-4

Price: $19.99

GET THE MONEY YOU NEED TO PAY FOR COLLEGE!

- Insider tips from top scholarship winners and judges
- Secrets to writing applications and essays that win
- Where to find the best scholarships
- Techniques for maximizing your financial aid package

Get Free Cash for College

ISBN: 978-1-61760-159-0

Price: $19.99

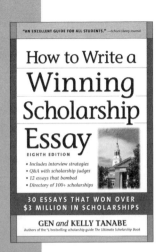

YOU WIN OR LOSE A SCHOLARSHIP WITH YOUR ESSAY AND INTERVIEW.

NOW YOU WILL LEARN HOW TO ACE BOTH!

- Complete instructions on crafting a powerful scholarship essay

- 30 money-winning essays that won $3 million in scholarships

- Scholarship judges reveal what separates a winner from a runner-up

- 12 essays that bombed and how to avoid their mistakes

- Master the interview with sample questions and answers

How to Write a Winning Scholarship Essay

ISBN13: 978-1-61760-161-3

Price: $17.99

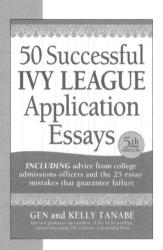

CRAFT A WINNING ESSAY
FOR AN IVY LEAGUE COLLEGE

- How to select the best topic
- What Ivy League admissions officers want to see in your essay
- The 25 mistakes that guarantee failure
- The top tips from Ivy League students on how to write a successful essay

50 Successful Ivy League Application Essays

ISBN: 978-1-61760-156-9

Price: $14.99

GET MORE TOOLS AND RESOURCES AT SUPERCOLLEGE.COM

Visit www.supercollege.com for more free resources on college admission, scholarships, and financial aid. And, apply for the SuperCollege Scholarship.

ABOUT THE AUTHOR

Joyce Slayton Mitchell is a top college advisor worldwide. Her book, *8 First Choices*, has more endorsements from top college admissions deans than any other college guide. Currently, She lives in China, New York City, and Vermont consulting with Chinese college businesses, and writing college guides, blogs, and newspaper columns on college admissions.

Ms. Mitchell has served as the Director of College Advising at independent schools in New Jersey, New York City, and a public school in Greenwich, Connecticut. Her mission in life is to help teenagers broaden their options as they take ownership for making their decisions about college and career.

Ms. Mitchell served on the Editorial Advisory Board for the College Board's College Board Review, on the school committee of *U.S. News & World Report's* special college issues, and is currently on the advisory board of the Council for Education Exchange (CIEE). She is the author of 42 works of nonfiction, including *Who is This Kid? Colleges Want to Know! Writing Exercises for Winning Applications* (Critical Thinking Co., 2019), *College Cultures: What's My Match?* (Ebook on Amazon, Itunes, Nook, 2012), *Winning the Heart of the College Admissions Dean* (Ten Speed Press, 2002, 2005), *Paris by Pastry: Stalking the Sweet Life on the Streets of Paris* (Jones Books, 2006, Ebook in press), *The Bible Express: The Fast Track to the Old and New Testaments* (Ambassador Press, 2006, Ebook, 2012), and *Belly Up to the Bar: Dining with New York City's Celebrity Chefs Without Reservations* (Cumberland House, 2008). She writes a college advice column in the *Hardwick Gazette* (Vermont), and in the *China Daily's* teen edition, *21st Century*, for Mainland China's national school students.

Ms. Mitchell travels extensively throughout the United States, Europe, China, and South Korea giving workshops, lectures, and seminars on subjects related to getting into college.